Tales of Victorian Headcorn or

The Oddities of Heddingden

A chield's among you taking notes
And, faith, he'll prent it

Burns

1909. Penelope Rivers aged 64

Tales of Victorian Headcorn

or

THE ODDITIES OF HEDDINGDEN

by

Penelope Rivers

Foreword by

Mary C.C. Horsfall

MERESBOROUGH BOOKS
1985

Published by Meresborough Books, 7 Station Road, Rainham, GILLINGHAM, Kent. ME8 7RS.
A list of titles available from Meresborough Books is printed at the end of this book.

ISBN Hardback 0948193050
Paperback 0948193069

Printed by Whitstable Litho Ltd., Whitstable, Kent.

CONTENTS

Aunt Penelope in old age. Holding the stage from the centre of the tennis court.

A TWENTIETH CENTURY FOREWORD

A year or two ago I was handed a bundle of papers by a now deceased relative who suggested that I might like to "have a look through these before you put them on the bonfire".

None of those papers reached any bonfire, and among the many treasures I found was a handwritten manuscript bound in red leather with its title standing out prominently in gold.

This then was my first sighting of 'The Oddities of Heddingden' by Penelope Rivers. I opened the book and read of her "visits to distant cottages, lantern in hand", I read her description of Christobel and Keturah Dudley in their dimity capes and muslin-covered mushroom hats, I saw references to family prayers and a "bed candle" and it seemed time to share these pictures of Victorian Kent.

With little difficulty I translated Heddingden into Headcorn and Penelope Rivers into Ellen M. Poole, my great-aunt Nellie. In choosing her pseudonym she had taken the Christian name Penelope, which I believe to be a fictitious variation of her nickname Aunt Pen, this perhaps because she usually had a pen in her hand to write or draw. The surname Rivers is presumably a play on her own surname Poole.

This is only the beginning of her playful deception. She assures us in her foreword that her sketches of Headcorn inhabitants are "literally and absolutely true" and this we must believe. But she has done all in her power to disguise her subjects and tease the reader. There may well be people living in Headcorn today who have the same name as her characters, in which case I would suggest that this is merely a coincidence. Penelope took great pains to conceal the identity of those people of whom she wrote, and when in Chapter IX she writes of Miss Vandeleur she actually goes to the trouble of altering the second vowel until she has worked her way through all five, and we find ourselves with Vandaleur, Vandileur, etc.

Welford Vicarage, birthplace of Ellen M. Poole, 'Aunt Penelope'.

However, as far as I can tell she has not altered local place names, and cannot be blamed for a contemporary postcard describing Pell Bridge as Church Walk. Houses and places of local interest will be recognised though they will be nameless.

It was by pure chance that I came upon her old home. After the size and elegance of the vicarage at Welford in Northamptonshire, where she was born and lived for over thirty years, she might well have regarded her new home as a "cottage", and I had not expected the very attractive and sturdily-built semi-detached house, still with the remains of the "triangular bit of lawn" in front and still with her beloved garden at the rear. The house has altered very little and the cellar still floods. Even after the construction of much new building the accoustics are still unusual, and sounds of traffic, people and animals are still exaggerated. The swishing of the sails of White Mill on the opposite side of the road, which was demolished in 1952, would have been clearly audible to her, so nothing seems to have changed since Penelope wrote that "much of the conversation of the passers-by reached me as I sat at work".

The subjects of her illustrations have altered little, save in one or two instances. She used a good deal of artist's licence in her pencil drawing of The Moat Farm, removing a line of willows which stood between flood-meadow and The Moat Farmhouse, and foreshortening the distance to the church. I regard this as one of her worst oversights, and she could have better shown this lovely, still partially-moated house, believed to have been built in about 1500 and one of the oldest in Headcorn. The site is alleged to date from Roman times, and has a flood-meadow still cobbled beneath the turf for cooling the feet of horses at the end of a day's work. The great Moat Farm wooden barns were burnt down in 1967 and all that remains is the base of the two oasts.

The postcards of Church Walk and The Old Footbridge are, as previously mentioned, Pell Bridge. Once known as Cloth House Walk a footpath leads from the bridge, over the railway line, past a mounting block and into the village. This was the route taken by wool traders bringing their produce to Headcorn from Cranbrook and neighbouring villages, and it is believed that it was originally wide enough to take a horsedrawn vehicle. The large slabs of Bethersden marble leading to the bridge are still lying exactly as they were nearly a hundred years ago.

The old oak has clearly deteriorated recently, and although in outline it has changed little since the time of Queen Victoria it is now black and sodden after a fire started by a gang of youths in 1983. Happily churches do not alter, and Penelope's picture of the fourteenth century parish church of St Peter and St Paul is the same today save that the spire on the north-east corner of the castellated bell tower has been removed, and the porch is now approached by an avenue of chestnuts planted to commemorate Queen Victoria's Diamond Jubilee.

The Schoolhouse, built in 1870 and attached to the old school, was the home of Joanna, Penelope's sister. It has changed very little but the bell tower has gone. Also little changed is the fifteenth century Old Workhouse, originally a clothworkers' hall and now used for commercial purposes. Penelope's illustration shows a low stone wall topped with iron railings running from this heavily timbered building along the front of the churchyard. These railings were removed during the Second World War and there is now no sign of the wall.

Nothing now remains of the four windmills in the village. White Mill, already mentioned, was the last to go, with the Black Mill being demolished not long before, much to the dismay of the local people. The only sign of a windmill now is that depicted on the village sign, which is to be seen frequently in Headcorn.

Penelope's postcard of Manor Farm now shows Manor Farm Cottage, and does not seem to have altered at all other than in the clearance of an overgrown hedge along the roadside. There is very little change too in The Old Vicarage, now Headcorn Manor. This lovely old Wealden hall house was built on the western edge of the churchyard as a parsonage in the late fifteenth century, where an earlier building on the same site, established in the thirteenth century, had been inhabited by priests.

In introducing Penelope to a late twentieth century Headcorn I have left her original manuscript unaltered save for the removal of unnecessary spelling errors, and a few words which are spelt in a different way nowadays and which would interfere with a reader's concentration. Words such as gypsey, stript, brouse, shew, stirdy, slipt and dropt have gone, although I have left one or two reminders of a more restful age such as erst, loath, weasand, verily, overweening and wight. Her handwriting was exceptionally good, steady and uniform throughout and remarkably easy to read.

Mention of a washing machine is surprising. This would have been a lidded wooden drum with a handle attached, at the end of which would have been a paddle. Turning the handle would have moved the washing round, past rubbing boards fitted to the sides, and although primitive to today's housewife it was probably more efficient than long hours of labouring at a stone sink. Also surprising is Penelope's mention of "the hire system", long before one imagines any organised hire purchase schemes had been thought of.

A word is perhaps advisable on the subject of the number of so-called lunatics with whom she came into contact. In her day I believe it is right to say there was a line drawn between the sane and the insane, and those who were not sane were speedily despatched to the nearest asylum, the only safe place for those afflicted. No allowance seems to have been made for mere eccentricity. Nowadays with vastly improved medical knowledge and the health service, a comforting visit from a doctor, with perhaps a prescribed tonic, sedative or course of corrective pills, would have been all that was necessary to put the matter right.

Ellen M. Poole, alias Penelope Rivers, was born at Welford Vicarage, near Northampton, on 9th November 1845. She was the younger daughter of George Ayliffe Poole and Susannah née Wilkes, my great-grandparents. George Ayliffe was a prolific writer and published many books, mostly on church architecture and Biblical subjects, but of more general interest were his innumerable water colour paintings and pencil sketches. On many of these sketches he collaborated with Susannah, and their minuscule signatures are both to be found hidden along the lower edges of their exquisite drawings.

It is believed that she went to live in Headcorn in 1887 and her sister Juliana, alias Aunt Joanna, followed a few months later. When a family dies out, as mine has, there are regretfully so many questions which were never asked and should have been, and so many answers given and now forgotten, but I believe these two spinster sisters were very happy living in the village for twenty years. By today's standards they frequently appear to be busy-bodies and unacceptably snobbish, but bearing in mind Penelope's amateur efforts at authorship, and viewing the results of their labours, they both seem to have contributed a good deal to the well-being of Headcorn. Their days there ended in 1907, when Juliana became very frail after an accident to her eyes, and together they went to live at Ightham where Juliana died on 14th April 1908.

Not a great deal more can be told about Ellen. Some time later she left Kent and went to live at St Swithin's Vicarage at Quinton near

Stratford upon Avon, where her cousin Gordon Hugh was vicar and lived with his parents, two sisters, a brother and a sister-in-law.

I remember paying a visit to the vicarage at a very early age and being greatly in awe of all these tall, gaunt and very silent people, but sadly these relatives of mine were elderly and this large household gradually broke up.

Ellen herself broke her hip, after which she was confined to a wheelchair. She was a popular visitor to my home, where she occupied the dining room and we ate our meals elsewhere. I have a very clear recollection of crouching beneath the staging of the conservatory which led out of her bedroom while she invented endless stories for me. Her favourite occupation on a fine day was to be wheeled to the centre of the tennis court, to hold the stage and be in command of our large garden while laughing and chatting to anyone within earshot.

She died in late July 1930 and is buried at Quinton with other members of her family.

I hand Penelope over to you now – Eleanor, John and little Bethany, and other children of Headcorn who I hope still know how to "make rabbits of their pocket handkerchiefs". Read all about this lady and the strange folk she met in your village.

And when you grow up you too must write of the people you meet, because in a hundred years time there will be new generations who will want to know yet more of the

'Oddities of Heddingden'.

Mary C.C. Horsfall
May 1985

DEDICATION AND FOREWORD

In an old oak chest, belonging to a parish which shall be nameless, among registers and other papers pertaining to village matters, is still to be seen the following letter, bearing the date 30th May 1679 and inscribed:

"For GoodMan Groomery at his house in . . ." (here follows the name of the parish to which he belonged and the street in which he lived) "Whereas the parishioners of . . . have had intelligence that you intend to make your habitation there they therefore thought good to declare to you that they utterly and altogether dislike thereof: and therefore desire you not to put yourselfe to that trouble and Charge to remove thither, for that they apprehend the law will not permit you to continue there without their consent, therefore would have you to prevent that trouble that will certainly ensue if you come thither. This is all from those who shall continue your friends (while you remain where you are)."

Below are the signatures of certain parish worthies who thus make it clear that their friendship can only be secured by the unfortunate person absenting himself from their neighbourhood.

What was the objection to GoodMan Groomery? There is no note to explain, but it is plain that for some cause his presence was distasteful to the inhabitants of the parish to which he had intended to migrate.

There are persons to whom anything outré or fantastic in the character or manners of their fellow creatures seems as disagreeable as was the presence of the ill-starred GoodMan Groomery to the parishioners of . . . To others however who do not desire that every man should be rolled into the exact facsimile of his neighbour as though he had passed under the hands of the doctor's assistant, this very eccentricity has an attractive quality. To them there is a saving grace in oddity, as in humour, that the ordinary person lacks.

To these last then I dedicate these sketches, which in spite of the appearance of exaggeration are literally and absolutely true.

The *appearance* of exaggeration is however inevitable. It arises from the necessity of taking each character out of that setting of the commonplace in which we all of us move, and results in a lack of proportion. Thus these sketches cannot pretend to be a true picture of *Life*; but they are, as I reiterate, a true picture of individuals with whom I have been personally acquainted and with many of whom I have made very real and pleasant friends.

The Oddities of Heddingden.

Chapter I.

"Odd & uncommon characters are the game I look for, & most delight in." Sir Roger de Coverley.

g: 1909- Some years ago, our niece who was staying with us in our Kentish village of Heddingden anounced her in:tention of writing a book, to be called "The oddities of Heddingden" -

Knowing that the village could boast more than the usual amount of "Cranks", I replied "Oh do, & let me read it".

"No, Aunt Penelope" was the answer, for you and Aunt Joanna will head the list!" -

The book to the best of my belief never has been, nor is ever likely to be begun by her; so before I get too old to tell the tale myself I have made up my mind to do so - Only neither Aunt Joanna nor I will figure in it except as lookers on at the oddities, strange doings, or kindlinesses of our neighbours.

Chapter I

HEDDINGDEN

"Odd and uncommon characters are the game I look for, and most delight in."

Sir Roger de Coverley

August 1909

Some years ago our niece, who was staying with us in our Kentish village of Heddingden, announced her intention of writing a book to be called 'The Oddities of Heddingden'.

Knowing that the village could boast more than the usual amount of cranks I replied, "Oh, do, and let me read it."

"No, Aunt Penelope," was the answer, "for you and Aunt Joanna will head the list!"

The book, to the best of my belief, never has been nor is ever likely to be begun by her. So before I get too old to tell the tale myself I have made up my mind to do so. But neither Aunt Joanna nor I will figure in it except as lookers on at the oddities, strange doings, or kindlinesses of our neighbours.

Our villagers, like many others in that neighbourhood, are very proud of being 'Men of Kent' and of a quality which they believe to belong exclusively to themselves, being impossible to coerce. Or, as they express it, they "can be led, but not driven". The latter part of the proverb is certainly true; of the former I am not so sure.

They stick to old names, old customs and old words. 'Witty' is still used as it was by the son of Sarach to mean wise, and his very expression of 'a witty child' is often used to describe a precocious youngster.

A mother, as she wiped a tear from her eye, told me of a little one whose life, when it was called away, had numbered months but not years. "It was a witty little thing and knowed its little bottle, it did, and its little saucepan, as well as well."

On one occasion a woman told me that her husband did 'terrify her' for coming to the Bible class. This sounded to my Midland county ears much like persecution and I was prepared to give rather horrified sympathy, till I found that it expressed the kindly 'chaff' of a husband who still treated his elderly wife like a lover. 'No bounds' implies that great things may be expected of the person under discussion, and the housewife still makes a 'gabardine' for her husband to do rough work in, such as hedging and ditching. We still give 'rough music' to a couple who quarrel, i.e. meet outside their house with kettles, pans, cow-horns, etc to drum them out of town, and in cases of gross immorality the actors are carried in effigy round the village in a donkey cart and burnt on Guy Fawkes' Day.

Nay other things than immorality (unpopularity, though it be only the unpopularity of the moment) may be visited in the same way, and not twenty years ago our good hardworking vicar was brought to his own door on the 5th of November, properly dressed in surplice and stole, carried round the parish and burnt, with much jubilation, by the side of 'the old Pope'.

Being busy at the moment, and unconscious of the design of the mummers, he sent out a shilling to the 'bonfire boys' and was not aware till the next day of the honour they had done him. In fact the whole display of animosity failed signally of its aim, as *he* did not discover the part he had played in it till the *day* after, and I never heard till a *year* after that I too was carried in procession and consigned to the fire, in the attitude of one weeping over his grave.

The fact is that my sister and I were both mixed up in the vicar's quarrel, and so for the time being shared his unpopularity. He had made a rule that the ringers were to attend church once, on the Sunday on which they rang, and I had expressed the opinion that the vicar was quite right, and that to ring others in to church and stay out themselves was disgraceful; and my sister had lent a set of handbells to the new ringers.

The Heddingden folk are great letter writers, and soon after this a postcard was delivered to each of us. My sister's was addressed to 'The Woman who does the parson's dirty work'. What it said I do not remember; I only remember that it was abusive without being witty. And mine missed a great opportunity, considering that it was my *tongue* that had erred, of some allusion to being "heavily clappered" and remarked that "I was not fit to live", that I "deserved to be hung by the neck as a scarecrow". It ended with "Mind how I catch you out at night!"

The Village in 1888, from 'Rambling Sketches of Headcorn' by Louis Wain, showing the rear of Clothworkers' Hall, now Shakespeare House.

As I was in the habit of attending evening classes, services, etc I expected that some dark night someone would probably jump out of the hedge and say "Bo!" But nothing happened and we went quietly and undismayed on our way, and probably disappointed the writers by taking no notice whatever of the cards and not trying to find out who were responsible for them.

All this is altered now, and I am writing of a time nearly twenty years ago, when the village had been stirred for good and evil by a Mission which left a lasting mark upon the character of the people.

Many fathers and mothers of families brought their children, and came themselves to be baptised and confirmed, and became regular and earnest communicants. Bible classes were started for men, women, girls and boys, and the spiritual life of the parish was visibly deepened. But of course with the 'moving of the waters' the mud was stirred also, and one instance of this came to my knowledge in a disconcerting manner when I proposed starting a Bible class for men.

I went first to two men of whom I felt nearly sure. One was a great Bible reader of a kind common among a certain school. He knew where to look for every text, could tell you how many times the number seven was mentioned, how often 'I am' came in both Old and New Testaments and what was the shortest text in Scripture. He had been a dissenter but was confirmed as a result of the Mission. He at once promised to join, and my next visit was made to a man who had taken an immense interest in the Mission and from whom I expected as ready an assent as from my textualist friend. I found myself however quite mistaken; he shook his head and said, "I shan't come if it's going to be like the last Bible class," and I then learned for the first time that after the Mission a good man and his wife had started a class for men.

They had laid themselves out in every way to make it attractive and had provided coffee each time, with the result that a lot of young fellows had joined it, egged on if not actually bribed by a man who was set against the Mission. They had spilt the coffee on the carpet, put out the lamp, thrown the Bibles at their teacher's head and ended by opening the window and having beer and cigars handed in.

I confess to having felt rather appalled when I heard this, but I had made up my mind to start the class and determined to go through with it whatever happened. "It is just such men as you that I want," I said to my doubtful friend. "Come, and stand up for me, and no such thing can happen." No, he would not promise, he would "see first how it answers".

I made several visits to distant cottages, lantern in hand, at an hour when I knew I should find the men at home, and some seemed inclined to come. But none, save the first one to whom I had spoken, would promise to do so.

The night – my birthday night – came, pitch dark and pouring with rain, and three men turned up: my doubtful friend, a drunkard helped by the Mission and one more, but *not* the only one on whom I had relied. We sang hymns and had a little talk, but I offered no coffee, and told them plainly that I would not stand any rudeness or bad behaviour. I did not think any of the men would treat a lady as they had treated the Mission helper, and I was right. The class grew till I had between twenty and thirty members and I never had the slightest trouble.

The men were mostly middle aged and fathers of families. Some were grandfathers. Only a few young unmarried men joined, but there were a few, and I never was treated with anything but courtesy and kindness. They brought me fruit, vegetables and flowers from their own gardens. Sometimes the contents of a red pocket handkerchief consisting of what they called 'ruts' (roots), carrots, turnips and parsnips were laid on the table. A bunch of violets came shyly down a coat sleeve and was smuggled into the hand of a young friend who used to play the hymns for me, and one old man would turn his back to me and say, "Feel in my tail pockets", and I would bring out half a dozen new laid eggs. They were a kindly generous set and I got very fond of them.

But it took some courage to enter a room 12 feet by 14 feet in which twenty men had been sitting, who came in freshly blacked boots and coats in which they had dried hops and who, after working all day in the fields had only washed hands and face and who had moreover put out their pipes on the doorstep. The mixed odours of black shag, blacking, hops and humanity were terribly overpowering and an open window was not to be thought of. Sometimes I ventured to open a crack behind the closely drawn curtains, but it was always found out. An old man who had the armchair near the window would put up his hand to shield his head and say, "I think, ma'am, there's a bit of a *drarft*," and my poor little attempts at ventilation were frustrated.

I always took care to be in the room to receive them one by one, both to get to know them better and also because if I came in when all were assembled it was more than I could stand. As it was, the used up air always gave me a hot head and cold feet, and I generally ended with a headache.

But in spite of all drawbacks I looked forward to Monday nights with great and increasing pleasure. This does not include the first Monday, which I awaited with inward trembling though with outward calmness, and I have seldom been more thankful than I was that night when my three men departed with no attempt on anyone's part to turn my little dining room into a bear garden.

The men were amusingly outspoken. On one occasion I was consulting them as to the best hour at which my three Bible classes for men, women and girls, should meet for a social evening. I suggested seven, but was met with dissent from one of the men who said, "No, it must be earlier than that. Mrs So-and-so said last time, 'If old Mother Rivers (myself) keeps my daughter out so late again I shan't let her go another time'." We had broken up at ten and the elders had seen the girls safely home, so I had not expected this rebuff!

Another of my men, in trying to persuade a neighbour to join the class, told me he had said, "You should go and hear that woman, she has a good understanding." He was an old man and might well have been my grandfather, but he called himself my 'eldest son', while a dear old woman of nearly eighty dubbed herself my eldest daughter.

At one of these annual teas my sister and I dressed up and introduced ourselves as two old women from our Midland country home. We covered our teeth with our lips and talked broad Northamptonshire. At first the audience were completely taken in, but after a time it began to dawn upon them who we were, and it was whispered that "it is the Miss Riverses but they have taken out their teeth!"

Curiously enough my sister and I did not live together. I had settled in the village first to help the vicar, and it was not till some

A Victorian postcard of Pell Bridge, then Church Walk.

Identical photograph taken in 1985, approached by the same flagstones but a now massive tree at the far end.

Louis Wain's sketch of Pell Bridge in 1888.

months later that I was followed by my sister Joanna, who brought with her from an orphanage she had started in Oxfordshire half a dozen boys and settled with them in our disused church schoolhouse. I had come the Advent before to help in the Mission, and after doing so had decided if I could get a house I would stay as lay helper.

When first I saw the house I eventually took, all the ceilings were on the floor. There was hardly a door or window that would open or shut, the garden was a piece of waste ground without so much as a cabbage or a currant bush, and the two-inch lawn was hardly to be distinguished from the untidy and muddy path. And when I settled in, buttercups were the only flowers I could get for the dinner table which, as my servant remarked, "would really be quite pretty *if they were not so common*"!

I was my own gardener, and my men took an immense interest in my performances, brought me plants, were very proud of my success and were most anxious that I should compete for prizes at the Cottage Gardeners' Show. They were also sympathetic on the rickety state of my house, and promised to come in a body and dig me out if it fell and buried me in the ruins.

I have just (September 1909) heard that the present tenants have had to turn out hastily, bag and baggage, as the house is pulling two

Aunt Penelope's home in 1985, with her 'beloved garden' at the rear.

ways and is declared to be positively unsafe. I had been much amused early in my tenancy with some lines I met with, which appeared to me to describe my position to a T:

> There was a man who had a house
> And when the winds began to rumble
> He with his shoulder propt it up
> For much he feared his house would tumble.
>
> He propt it up throughout the day
> Until 'twas time to go to bed,
> But when he put his candle out
> The house fell down upon his head.

I have handed on this description to my successors, to whom it is I fear proving only too true.

No account of the parish at this time would give a fair idea of it without mention of the Sunday school. When our vicar had come two years before, he found one devoted old lady who went Sunday after Sunday and kept together a little band of twelve children. When my sister and I came, there were 120 children and twelve teachers, mostly tradesmen's or farmers' daughters from fourteen to eighteen years old, though the good old lady who had so bravely continued her work of love in loneliness and discouragement still taught her class as usual.

The children were a rough lot and difficult for such young teachers to cope with. Sticks were forbidden but were often brought into school, and used to thwack the desks with at opportune moments when the teacher's back was turned. Pockets were filled with acorns or chestnuts, which when discreetly aimed annoyed the teacher without exposing the culprit to punishment, as it was hopeless to try and discover whose hand had thrown the missile. Pins bent in a skilful triangle with the point sticking up, would sit invitingly on the seat or desk and stab the unwary, and over this disorderly rabble I was appointed superintendent.

Happily I was no novice, having taught from the time I was twelve years old, and I was commonly supposed to be gifted with 'eyes behind'. A boy in my father's parish years before had asked my sister whether she or I were going to sit with the children in church that Sunday, and when he found that it was she he had remarked that he was glad as she was not so 'viciouslike' as Miss Penelope.

The old postcard above shows Pell Bridge with old oak handrail. Below is the same scene today with 'hollow iron rods', see p.28.

'Viciouslike' I had to be at Heddingden, and I waged long though in the end successful war against sticks. The boys would come in looking like perfect saints, with a stick concealed up the sleeve or in the leg of their trousers, and a sudden startling thwack would make the whole school jump. One had to go the rounds before school began, demand the sticks separately, break them up and feed the fire with them, or better still make the boy himself convert them into fuel. Many plans were tried to evade the law and tire out the superintendent, and on one occasion a stick was so readily and cheerfully given up that it did not need much discernment to discover that some hidden triumph was expected on the part of the owner as he drew it forth, and placed in my hand the straightest, toughest and thorniest briar ever grown. Being prepared it was easy to grasp it without suffering from its thorns and to consign that also to the fire. That was I think the last attempt to bring the forbidden articles into school. But the behaviour in church was too irreverent to be borne.

The ringers themselves, with singular infelicity, put their hats and pipes in the font as they went by. What wonder that their children had no feeling for the sacredness of the building, nor any idea of devotion during the service.

The boys brought comic papers to church and read them out loud during the service, made rabbits of their pocket handkerchiefs, and with an adroit movement sent them all along the line of children to a chosen friend who, at a convenient moment, returned them. Knives, marbles, pencils and various other treasures were brought out of their pockets and served as playthings during the service, until a fiat went out that whatever the superintendent once confiscated, however valuable, was never returned. A very few Sundays of annexation, when it was discovered that the superintendent stuck to her word, had a magic effect. But no one knelt, no one thought of bringing a prayerbook and *devotion* was indeed as far off as ever.

A one armed man, once a dissenter and with no more reverence than was to be expected from his bringing up, was supposed to keep over a hundred ill-behaved children in order, and signally failed. So a meeting was called of all the young teachers, and the suggestion made that each should sit with her own class, find the places for them in their prayerbooks, and get if possible something like attention at least.

Some friends gave 120 hassocks, the teachers made a little collection to provide twopenny prayerbooks, and we began our crusade.

Old postcard of the Moat Farm barns which were burnt down in 1967. All that now remains are the bases of the two oasts. In the foreground is the flooded meadow of the Moat Farm House. Below: a recent photograph shows the flood meadow dry.

The teachers at first were very loath to try the experiment, until the superintendent promised that if at the end of three months no improvement was visible she would set them free.

An old man in the congregation remarked that we reminded him of 'the noble army of Martyrs' and the suggestion was not inapt.

Well, we prospered more or less, and the children improved very slowly but still surely, and we even got a certain amount of eagerness for the possession of a prayerbook, but the reign of the twopenny prayerbooks ended somewhat prematurely.

Every Sunday they were religiously collected by the teachers and tidily piled on what I believed to be a rather majestic ventilator, till the first Sunday in November, when we were greeted on entering the church with a curious and overpowering smell of burnt American cloth, and I discovered to my dismay that my ventilator was really a stove, and the prayerbooks were all baked crisp and brown and crackled to pieces when taken from their place. Thus ended our little scheme for providing the means for intelligent behaviour, but it had done its work and cremation was not an inglorious end to it, as from its ashes sprang the desire to possess and bring prayerbooks of their own to church, and a few out of the many really tried to follow the service.

Our parish, though not what is generally called pretty, is eminently picturesque, and one could hardly go a quarter of a mile in any direction without finding some little bit that lent itself to the pencil or brush. Willow bordered ponds, huge red tiled barns with massive doors and spacious interiors, old timbered houses, in some of which the upper storey is like the crypt of a cathedral. The king posts stand free, being almost as large and dignified as stone pillars, and the sloping roof is as beautiful in its way as the ribbed or groined roof of the crypt. Odd bits of fourteenth or fifteenth century carving are to be found in the spandrels of the arches, and oak doors, studded with nails and guarded with wooden bars, keep out the intruder.

The Flemish cloth workers have left their mark in the 'Halls' where they plied their trade. Some are high pitched and deep eaved with great chimneys, others are low and covered with creepers, but all are lovely in form, and the mellowness of age still remains, to show what the village must have been before the reign of ugliness began with the modern builder.

We had an old oak bridge, supported on massive stone piers, and I do not know that our people are greater barbarians than their fellows, but it would be difficult to exceed the barbarity of substituting

Ellen M. Poole's pencil drawing of Moat Farm in 1893.

hollow iron rods for the beautiful oak handrail and flat slabs for the strong beams of which the footway of the bridge was built. Or the crowning of the parapet of a fine old stone bridge, which spans our tiny stream a little further up, with pink cement! This latter bridge is an historic one, having been built by Stephen Langton to facilitate his journey from his archiepiscopal See of Canterbury to his Palace at Mayfield.

The long line of flagstones at either end of the wooden bridge are still left to serve the purpose of stepping stones when our usually shallow brook swells with continuous rain, or a sudden thunderstorm turns it in to a roaring torrent to overflow all its banks.

There grew – for the stream has been 'cleaned out' and with it, I fear, many of the beautiful water plants that once made it a thing of beauty – the stately spearwort six or eight feet high, a mass of gold and green among the sedges, together with arrowhead, and flowering rush, and sheets of water ranunculus. In the ponds, of which there are over three hundred in the parish, grow bog bean and water violet, yellow and white water lilies and frogbit, whorled water-milfoil and the yellow iris, and over the flat stretches of hop gardens one gets

This old postcard shows interior of the Parish Church of St Peter and St Paul. The intricately carved rood screen was the full width of the church until destroyed in the sixteenth and seventeenth centuries by puritans or reformers.

most lovely sky effects with here and there a mill standing out gaunt and solemn against the sunset.

It is a sight never to be forgotten when the hops are gathered and wagons with three or maybe four horses stand loaded with the purple-brown vines, and the hop poles are stacked like the tents of an encamping army while here and there a remnant of the yet green hop still flutters from a neglected pole. Rooks peck at the last morsel of seed as it lies on the ground and the September mist wraps it all in a poetic veil. And yet I have heard Heddingden called 'an ugly place'.

Our church is a fine one in its way but much despoiled. Remnants of especially beautiful perpendicular glass still remain in the upper tracery of the north windows, and the base of a fine rood loft of deeply cut linen pattern with very good carving on the cornice speaks of a once beautiful screen, but in its present state it looks heavy and meaningless, the whole upper part with its probable fan tracery having been ruthlessly cut away.

Last year (1908) a portion of the screen, that of the Lady Chapel, was beautifully restored by private benefaction. It is to be hoped that the parishioners will have the taste to see how greatly it has added

Recent photographs showing the old oak tree in a far more serious state of dilapidation than a century ago.

The old oak tree a hundred years ago, before the wanton damage of 1983.

to the dignity of their parish church, and that before long the screen may be carried across the chancel arch and the rood be restored to its original position.

A glorious old oak, once part of the original forest, now hollow with age but beautiful in decay, stands by the south porch, from the parvis of which a hunted priest once made his escape in its branches which then stretched over the porch. The tree is over a thousand years old, yet still every spring it puts forth a crown of green leaves and in autumn drops acorns that spring into verdant life. They are tender children of an ancient and honoured mother, for the 'Heddingden oak' is renowned throughout the county.

That the forest land was difficult to cultivate we still have evidence from some of the names of old holdings in the parish. We have 'Hunger Down', 'Starveden', 'Little Starveden', 'Starvegut' and 'Bedlams'. 'Noah's Ark' may tell of the time when floods were more common even than now, though I have waded above my shoe tops to a distant cottage as the result of a violent thunder shower and seen the big boys carrying the little children on their backs from school. And now October 1909 has added a tale of flood such as has not been known for thirty years, the water having nearly reached the ancient 'flood stone'.

'Dripping-pan field' one hopes may at least speak of dripping in the pan, but 'Gooseneck Lane' only describes the graceful curve of the stepping stones that make a dry footway to the church.

'Knave's Acre' and 'Convict Cottages, Shyaway Lane', though quaint, can hardly be called encouraging names, and it is disappointing to find that 'Shyaway', though vividly descriptive of the loneliness and dreariness of its situation, is yet spelt 'Sheerway' and may probably only recall the name of the original owner. One wonders to what old custom 'Lording Tree' may point, and what can have been the origin of the word now corrupted into 'Pink-horn Green'. Someone suggests 'Pink thorn' but there are no thorns to give it the name, and as they are some of the longest lived of our trees the stumps at least would probably still mark the spot where they once blossomed. And I am doubtful – or perhaps *not* doubtful! – as to whether pink thorns were introduced into this country at as early a date as the name itself.

Old customs, as well as old names, hold their own, and mead is still made and drunk on some of the farms. This takes us back to our Viking forefathers, who must have had strong heads if they could drink in any quantity a beverage so luscious and heady, which in these degenerate days we should only produce in liqueur glasses.

Nor are old names and old customs the only ancient things that hold their own, but old superstitions also. The mother of a man yet living in the parish was feared as a witch, and an old woman told a friend of mine that she had herself seen her in the form of a white hare jump over a hedge and disappear.

We have a haunted house too, with a history that might have held its own with that of Miss Haversham in 'Great Expectations', where the funeral bake-meats still rot on the table – or rather I should imagine were long ago cleared away by rats, mice and black beetles – where tattered curtains blow through the broken lattice, and blinds grey with age hang crooked and disconsolate in the window frames. It has never been entered since the death of the last owner, a maiden lady of a certain age, who left in her Will her desire that nothing should be touched after her death, but that the house and all it contained should be left to natural decay.

It a little spoils the story from a ghostly aspect that the garden behind the house is still used. The house itself faces the street, and though the shrubs within the iron railings have been left unpruned from that day to this, they have not made so impenetrable a screen as to enhance the mystery to a gruesome extent and only once, from a frightened child, have I heard of the appearance of 'a face at the window'.

Old grudges too have been carried to an almost unbelievable pitch. Two old brothers, sons of the 'white hare' and brothers of the owner of the haunted house, did not speak to each other for twenty years, though they shared not only the same room but the same bed, and when they had business to transact they wrote to each other on the subject. It will not surprise anyone to hear that in the family of one of the brothers were three idiots, nor that the other brother, though Lord of the Manor, goes about in a dirty smock, loading his own dung carts. He is known by the name of 'Muck Meyrick'.

It is said, I fear with truth, that he does not even change his smock when he comes in to supper with his two nice daughters, to whom he has given a good education. He would, like his sister, have made a good subject for Dickens' pen, with his small cunning face set on a withered neck that issues from the loose collar of his smock like that of a tortoise. The face is withered as a weasand apple but has none of the rosy cheek, and the head is cocked on one side like a listening earwig.

Close to miserliness in most directions he will now and then do a generous act, but his sharp cunning eyes are not pleasant to look upon, and he has a terrible gift of silence that brings you up short like a dead wall if he does not choose to be approached. His wife had died when his daughters were three and four years old, and he and an ill-favoured housekeeper had brought them up between them. Happily he had sent them to a good school in a neighbouring town, but his coarse jokes and impenetrable silences were very trying to them on their return home. He did not make them happy and they were terribly afraid of him. Both ran away from home to be married, and the marriage of one at least was not a happy one. And though after a time he allowed them to come and see him he took no interest in their children, and would not allow either of the husbands to enter the house.

For some months before his death he suffered from a bad leg to which he would pay no heed, till a good nurse, who happened to be in the village, insisted on dressing it and keeping it clean. His end came suddenly. He went to a tithe dinner and ate, contrary to doctor's

Old postcard of Manor Farm showing the cottages attached to Rushford Manor.

orders, very heartily of everything before him, including a plate of pickles! He was taken ill that night, would obey no orders and was quite unmanageable. Delirium set in, followed by unconsciousness, and when his daughters came he did not know them. He died two days after.

When his daughters married he threatened to cut them off with a shilling and to marry again, but it was found that the only Will that he left was unsigned. So the daughters, as next of kin, came in to the neglected farm, to a bag of twenty pounds in silver, a few I.O.U.s and various scraps of paper on which sums lent were jotted down generally without date or signature. Many of these debts proved to be unrecoverable, and a few hundreds at the most were got in and these with difficulty. In February 1910 the farm is still on the market, and owing to its neglected state it will not realize all that it should be worth.

The funeral was a sad sight, as perhaps the old waggoner who was his contemporary, and had worked for the family all his life, was the only true mourner.

Near the porch of our parish church is an old tomb commemorating the members of a large family of the name of Chitty, some of whom lived at Heddingden and others at Lydgate in the same county. There lies the body of one Dame Chitty, a noted housewife to whom young

By 1985 the building had become two cottages, although the outline remained the same in a far less tranquil setting.

girls were 'bound' as servants by the parish Union. She is supposed to have overworked them, and been harsh if not actually cruel to them, and after her death her ghost still haunted the house where she had lived. All through the night there were sounds as if an army of servants was employed in scrubbing, sweeping and cleaning, and the rattling of pails and the splashing of water were accompanied by the strident voice of the Dame herself scolding the maids.

No one would sleep in the house and at length the Church was called upon to exorcise the ghost. This must have been about the year 1777. The then vicar of the parish assembled some of the clergy of the neighbourhood, and each holding a tall candle and praying fervently they awaited the appearance of the Dame. Candle after candle was extinguished by some unseen hand, but the vicar held on valiantly and continued to wrestle in prayer with the ghost, until his candle burnt down into the socket. After that Dame Chitty troubled the house no more.

They must have been an uneasy family as another Dame Chitty at Lydgate was also credited with 'walking'.

This legend was handed down to the present owner of the mill at Heddingden from his grandmother, who was housekeeper at the vicarage when the occurrence recorded took place.

Chapter II

THE DUDLEYS

"The eyes full of laughter, the throat of tears"

Peer Gynt, p.65

"What a strange place was this . . . in which gentlewomen had their lodging in so foul a place" *The Chaplain of the Fleet*

Were they ladies? This was the question we asked ourselves and each other as we followed them out of church one Sunday morning, and saw the quaint pair of sisters trotting before us arm in arm down the churchyard path.

I think it was I who decided that none but ladies would dare to appear in public in such a dress. Each sister wore a rusty black skirt, a short calico or dimity cape that reached the elbow, and was gathered with some attempt at coquetry into a rosette at the back. A cotton pocket handkerchief was knotted round the neck, their hair was twisted into a tight knob at the back of the head and they wore mushroom hats. These were covered with coarse white muslin, and a few scraggy flowers of real geranium and ears of corn were pinned round the crown. Even through the muslin one could see the chipped and broken edges of the straw brim, and the fact that they were burnt a dull brown could not be concealed.

The costume was completed by grey cotton gloves, too long in the fingers and too short at the wrist, and as one got to know them better one discovered that their clothes were chiefly pinned together. By some perverse freak of character, if any part of the dress was white it was generally held in place by a black safety pin, and if black it would be a white one. They never held up their skirts which wiped their shabby elastic-sided boots, and neither skirts nor boots ever came within hale of a brush.

I am aware that in this description I lay myself open to the accusation of exaggeration, but anyone who knew them would bear me out in it as strictly true.

Who were they? Where did they come from? And had they any friends?

Nobody knew. They took a small cottage, furnished it with old boxes and started a school. Furniture there was none. A basket chair, sent in by the vicar, was the only piece of furniture in the tiny sitting room. A couple of boxes, one on top of the other, served as a table, and another couple for two chairs. The room was bare of any ornament whatsoever. All this I saw at a glance when at the request of the vicar I called upon them.

Their names had a quaintness which fitted in with their appearance, and Christobel and Keturah Dudley came to be wellknown names in Heddingden.

When Keturah opened the door to me at my first call, she wore apparently as almost her only clothing a long Dolman cloak. One could see through the hanging sleeve the naked arm, and through the loose collar the bare throat and neck. But there was no sign of shyness or confusion in the manner in which she ushered me in and shouted to her deaf sister that this was 'Miss Rivers'. The one chair was brought forward for me, and the two sisters sat down each on her own box with as regal an air as if they had been thrones. They talked of books and of the news of the day, and entertained me with true courtesy and dignity.

How they lived, whether they had enough to eat and enough fire to warm themselves was a serious question. They generally peeped over the dingy half blind before they opened the door, and when very occasionally one caught a glimpse of the kitchen a battered teapot and an inconceivably dirty and untidy room was all that could be seen. The time came when I was admitted into this black hole, where never a window was opened nor a scrubbing brush used, as a familiar friend, but for some time the parlour with its array of boxes was as far as I penetrated.

They opened their school, and strange to relate people sent their children there, 'young ladies', daughters of farmers, shopkeepers and of the veterinary surgeon. And what is more they were taught so well that in time Christobel went daily to the vicarage to teach the vicar's four little sons, who all passed into public schools with éclat.

But they were *desperately* poor, and though clever with their brains they were absolutely incapable with their hands. Food was sent them but it was ill cooked and wasted. A chicken arrived one day in a hamper of good things, ready plucked and trussed, but by some extraordinary piece of mismanagement, in attempting to stuff it they put in acetic acid instead of salt and the fowl was useless. Clothes were also sent anonymously, and with due reference to their taste in dress, but they were never worn. Rich and poor brought offerings and everything was accepted with dignity and grace, but nothing seemed to help towards a less squalid existence. The old ladies were still pinned together with crooked black and white safety pins, still wore pocket handkerchiefs round their necks, and year after year the same hats covered with crumpled muslin appeared, whether it was summer or winter.

Hop-picking found them with a bin which they shared between them, but they were slow and clumsy at the work and did not earn enough to pay for the destruction of their clothes. And with hop-picking came a revelation. Keturah fainted at the bin, and a kind friend who saw her home found nothing in the larder but bread, and there were no coals in the house. Then too it was discovered that they had an old mother in an upstairs room for whom the poor things worked, but who too was evidently suffering from actual want of necessary food. Need I add that the friend so made continued to help them in every way, and that other friends redoubled their efforts on their behalf?

Several times one or another tried to get them into some sort of home for poor gentlefolk, but always with the same result. There was something – they never told what – in the simple questions asked on the application paper that they refused to answer.

Had their father committed some crime? Were they living under a false name? No one knew, and their reticence had so much of dignity in it that it was impossible to press them beyond the limit of good manners. But the endeavour to get them into a home was of course after the death of the poor old mother, which happened soon after her presence was discovered, accelerated, as the doctor affirmed, by want of nourishment.

As I stood by the grave with the sisters Keturah reeled, and would have fallen had not Christobel and I supported her. As we turned away she wrung her hands and wailed, "And no son to bury her!"

There was a brother then. Who and where was he? And why were these two poor women left to face life alone?

The same friend who had accompanied Keturah to her home from the hop garden found out much about their circumstances, but there was one subject on which they were silent and that was their mother. The brother was dead, they said, and apparently no tragedy was connected with him, but that there was a tragedy in their lives none could doubt. Afterwards one came to wonder whether the mother was insane. She had been kept in an upstairs room from the time they came to Heddingden and until the last stage of her illness no one saw her. I was only admitted to the bare room when she lay in the sleep of death, and whatever her secret was it died with her.

Bravely the sisters faced life again, with never an unkind word for anyone and full of interest and sympathy for other people's pleasures. When I saw their cheerless existence I hardly liked to tell them how much I was looking foward to my first trip abroad. But they were intensely interested, and only exacted a promise that when I returned from Norway I would describe all I saw and show them my sketches.

They kept their vivid interest in everything and always enjoyed an invitation to tea, though I never could get them to eat more than the fashionable couple of slices of thin bread and butter and a dainty cake. Were they so near starvation that they had no appetite? Or were they too proud to eat properly? I used to make an enormous meal of it myself to try and induce them to eat, but in vain.

I shall never forget one Christmas Day when I invited them to share my roast beef and plum pudding, and asked my sister and a friend to meet them. I begged the two latter to put on the least eveningified of their evening dresses that the poor ladies might not be put to the blush, when a rumour reached me that Keturah was going to appear in a low dress! I hurried off to tell my friends to put on all their frills and furbelows to greet them, and awaited the arrival of the two sisters with considerable interest.

The bell rang and I went into the hall to meet them. There they were, in the muslin hats, rusty waterproofs and the uncleaned elastic-sided boots. But as the butterfly breaks through the unseemly husk of the chrysalis, so did the sisters cast off their outer shell and emerge in all the glory of evening dress.

Nothing could make Christobel anything but plain, and a limp crêpe black dress with long streamers of white satin ribbon from neck and sleeves that nearly touched the ground did but add a grotesque touch to her appearance. But Keturah was positively handsome and might have been a duchess from her aristocratic bearing. Again one was forced to say "Who are they?"

The soft falling black silk dress cut low, with clean chiffon frilling which lay daintily against the white shoulders, a gold bracelet and a simple gold chain about the throat, and above all her abundant hair no longer done up in a hard knot at the back of the head, but well brushed and plaited into a coronet for the well shaped head, had absolutely transformed her. One saw in a revealing flash what she must have been as a girl, in the days of which they sometimes spoke, when their father was well off and they lived in luxury.

It was terribly pathetic. Surely she must have had much attention and probably many lovers. The fine profile, well turned neck and arms, hands that one could see must have been those of a lady though now roughened by hard and dirty work. What a pretty girl, what a handsome woman she must have been. Even Christobel, before a slight stroke had twisted the poor face and affected the speech, her dignified walk and fine manners told of days when she used to tread shallow stairs, and Turkey carpets, instead of tramping muddy roads in broken boots to teach little tallow chandlers at fourpence an hour.

For some years Keturah walked to and from a neighbouring parish four miles off, to teach three little children, and one day I found her with her foot not too tidily bandaged. I discovered that she had upset a saucepan of boiling water over it, and without even having it properly dressed had for some days been walking backwards and forwards to her pupils as usual.

I also saw the poor old couple on another occasion, weariness in every limb and still arm in arm, returning from the county town where they had been to choose a piano on the hire system on which to give lessons. The town was nine miles off, and the daily bus being beyond their means these poor old ladies had tramped the eighteen miles without a murmur.

And so it was a real pleasure to share our Christmas fare with people who so evidently appreciated the little festival. To be well dressed for once must have been in itself a treat, and the tiny present placed on each guest's plate was received with a grace that doubled the pleasure of giving.

The evening ended with carol singing in which the voices of the sisters joined, but I cannot say that they added to the effect. I do not think that at any time they can have had musical voices or a fine ear for tune.

Well, the Butterflies' Ball had to end as all things in this life must, and the resplendent wings were hidden once more under the shabby waterproofs, but I have always looked back upon that Christmas dinner with pleasure, in which amusement and sadness were blended, and they spoke of it with a rapture that was truly pathetic.

One wishes that one could end here but their last days at Heddingden were passed under a cloud, the memory of whose shadow abides with me yet.

It began to be whispered among the pupils that Miss Keturah was 'very strange'. Then neighbours spoke of violent quarrels between the sisters and strange noises at night, and it was even said that Keturah was heard dragging her sister downstairs by her hair and had threatened to throw her into the well. Once in church they had a stand up fight in which Keturah roughly pushed Christobel into her place and the clergyman had to interfere. Then one day I was suddenly told that she was to be taken to the asylum in an hour's time.

My poor old friends. What could I do? Clearly not interfere in any way with Keturah, but be ready to try and comfort Christobel when she was taken away. So with a beating heart and quaking limbs I went to the turn of the road from which I could see the Dudleys' house, and waited. I had not long to wait. A fly drove up with a policeman in plain clothes on the box and a nurse inside, and the sisters came down the path arm in arm to meet it.

Apparently they, or at any rate Keturah, were unaware of the meaning of it, and I saw Keturah draw back as the door was opened for her. Then with a cry she was lifted in. A torrent of bad language followed in her high strained voice and the fly drove off. Another moment and her hand was outside on the handle of the door, another and stronger hand was put over hers, the door was once more fastened and the fly turned the corner and was out of sight.

Before I could reach the cottage a kind neighbour had taken Christobel into her house and I followed, to find her rocking herself backwards and forwards, crying "*My* Kitty, *my* Kitty, I'd rather live with her mad than with anyone else sane."

When she saw me she rose up and said, "Take me home." We went, with the neighbour following with that unfailing source of comfort – a cup of tea. I left her at last in the neighbour's hands, somewhat quieted with the thought that there was more chance of recovery at an asylum than with the most loving care at home. I went on to the vicarage where the vicar, who had perforce been instrumental in getting Keturah taken away, was only waiting for her removal to go to the bereaved sister.

What followed I was not there to see but I heard it from him afterwards.

He was soothing Christobel, and trying to make arrangements that she should not be left alone that night when, with her head in the air and a look of concentrated hatred and disdain on her face as she passed him, in marched Keturah. The magistrate had failed to pass her as insane. The moment her attempt to escape from the fly had failed she had pulled herself together, sat rigidly still and collected, and behaved so absolutely like a person in full possession of her senses that the magistrate could not sign the necessary papers. That strange dignity which the sisters possessed in such a remarkable degree had come to her aid, and nothing could be done but to bring her back.

"Thank you, Mr Inspector, for a very pleasant drive" was her parting shot to the policeman, as she alighted at her own gate and sailed up the pathway to the door. Nothing could be done but to warn her that she would be watched, and any ill treatment of her sister noticed. After all their house was their castle, and as Christobel welcomed her home with delight they could but be left together.

For some time I kept away, fearing to make matters worse by a visit, but gradually things fell back into their old grooves. One day I found that the sisters had been twice to see me while I was out on a long round of parish visiting, so I went to their house at once. They had put an advertisement in the paper for a cottage and wanted to consult me as to the answers they had received. Among them was one from a cousin of my own who had a cottage to let and wanted two ladies to help in the parish!

What a traitor I felt as they placed the letter in my hands, for truth to tell he had written to me, knowing that they came from our parish, to ask if they were the kind of tenants he wanted. My reply, which would quench all their hopes, was already in his hands.

Happily he had only given initials in his answer to their advertisement so it told no tales. I preserved a discreet silence on the subject, only suggesting that it was a long way to go and did not sound to me suitable. A word sufficed to turn them and we consulted over a heap of other letters. School keeping or parish work was still what they were in search of, and what could one do? One could give no real help under such circumstances, and could only discuss the question as to whether each cottage mentioned sounded suitable or unsuitable to their purpose.

I left home for a few weeks and when I returned they were gone.

They had departed by the daily bus to our market town, carrying with them as personal luggage two dilapidated fish baskets. Their furniture, miserably poor at the best but no longer consisting only of boxes, was deposited with a station master down the line to be sent for when he received their address. Leaving no address behind them they disappeared from the Heddingden world, and would have done from all their friends in the neighbourhood had not the lady who had so long interested herself in them contrived to trace them to a different county and found friends for them there.

Every Christmas, in return for a small Christmas box, I receive a poetical effusion from Christobel, while both sisters write to their other friend. But we are sworn to secrecy as to their whereabouts and Heddingden knows them no more.

Chapter III

POLITE LETTER WRITERS

"There is sure another flood toward and these couples are coming to the Ark. Here comes a pair of very strange beasts"

Very different were the St. Johns, mother and daughter, who lived in a tiny house three minutes walk from the church in which they seldom worshipped. Very different in character but sadly alike, alas, in the fact that they and their house were nearly as dirty as the Dudleys.

But there was none of the cheerful kindly spirit which caused the Dudleys, with all their faults and oddities, to make and to keep friends.

Mrs St. John was a gentle complaining woman with not very strong health and getting on in years. Miss St. John's age it would be impossible to guess. If you walked behind her she might be anything from twenty-five to thirty-five, but when she turned round she might have been seventy. The countenance was an evil one. A wrinkled face with fierce eyes, a bad complexion and a hideous mouth from which one shrank as instinctively as from the dirt of her person and the unkempt house. She had one interest in life – a huge tabby cat – which she led by a string when she went out, and on which she lavished far more care and affection than on her mother, who I believe was absolutely afraid of her and her violent temper.

They had one servant who stayed with them for a year or two, and during her reign the house though dilapidated was habitable. But when she left they could get no one who would stay more than a week or two, as each in turn objected to having anything that came handy thrown at them! At last they took to doing, or not doing, their own work, and then the house was a veritable pigsty.

At the clergyman's request I went to see them, and tried to interest them in what was going on in the parish and to persuade the daughter to attend church. The poor old mother crept alone to the Holy Communion occasionally but the daughter was immovable. I tried to make friends with her, took a walk with her now and then, and tried to get her to talk of anything but her grievances which were many. But in vain, and when I mentioned to them, as before to the Miss Dudleys, that I was going to spend three weeks in Norway, a perfect rage of jealousy seemed to possess her. The mother maundered on with feeble complaints of the monotony of their existence while everyone else was able to indulge in a change. They spoke of poverty, but I found afterwards that they had considerably more than the joint incomes of my sister and myself. When I said goodbye Miss St. John's expression was a malediction.

On one occasion I went to ask them to take an interest in rescue work and a Home for the training of fallen girls in the neighbourhood, but in vain. "Why don't they go to church and read the Commandments; they're put up on the church wall," exclaimed the daughter, "I look upon them as dirt under my feet."

I ventured to suggest that it was fortunate for these poor women that Christ had not looked upon them in the same light, and so I left the house.

Not long after, the daughter of one of my Bible class women got into trouble and the mother, broken down with age and sorrow, had a serious illness. The case was a bad one, and the mother in speaking of it said, "The 'Old-un' got on my back and tempted me to send her to the Union." She resisted the 'Old-un's' suggestion and took care of the girl at home and then fell ill herself.

They lived next door to the St. Johns, so that my constant visits to the house were I suppose watched and commented on. However that may be my sister-in-law, who like the St. Johns was an Irish woman, came to stay with me, and I got her to call with me on my very unpleasant neighbours, and after knocking several times in vain we were about to turn away when the door of an outhouse opened and Miss St. John, with her cat on her arm and a look of perfect fury on her face, came out.

"I have brought a compatriot of yours to see you," I said, advancing to shake hands.

"What a beautiful cat," remarked my sister-in-law, willing to make friends.

No answer was returned to either remark, but looking straight at me and ignoring my sister-in-law altogether she said, "Are you going to see Mrs Brent?" (the sick woman next door).

"Not today," I replied.

"You'd better go then," she answered and banged the door in our faces.

The next day I received the following letter:

"Dear Miss Rivers,

"We are obliged to decline the acquaintance of any Advocate of your creditable friends Brents, against whom we contemplate taking legal proceedings. (The legal proceedings contemplated were for driving the cat out of their garden. P.R.) *You know plenty* of what we have to bear from them. Mrs Stone told you a good deal lately, or at least I told her to do so. Ask her if she did not. Pray do not trouble to answer this in *any way*.

"It is perhaps *safer* neither to write or talk much to *you* about it, as you are so absurdly infatuated with them, so don't come here!

faithfully yours,
Maria St. John

"P.S. You need never maintain that the elderly Brent female is not to blame, *for it is not the case*; she may say so, but she is a liar and a hypocrate! *We have interfered with these people in no way*; we have done nothing to them; never opened our lips or looked at them since Miss Brent produced her bastard. But that's our fault! *We* have had too much good feeling to patronize them or theirs.

"With reference to *your* wise choice of protegées, permit me to remind you as to what happens when pearls are cast before swine."

Happily they did not stay long after that. The cat died, which seemed to unsettle them. She carried it in a fly to the home of their old servant, saw it buried in her garden, sent her £1.0.0. a year to keep the grave in order, and so they departed regretted by few. But in justice to them I must say that after they were gone I found three people to whom they had been kind, the Miss Dudleys among the number.

Though I have given these people a place among 'The Oddities of Heddingden' both families were importations, but we were by no means lacking in strange characters whose fathers and grandfathers had never moved from the place. How long ago it was that a gipsy basket-maker with six cats had settled in the village I do not know, but she and hers were old inhabitants, and side by side with the wheedling manner and shrewd wit of the gipsy she possessed education and intelligence enough to read Shakespeare with avidity.

A few doors from her lived a cheerful old rag and bone woman who tramped the country for miles, pushing before her her little handcart of odds and ends, on which was generally seated her last adopted orphan. She wore a coal-scuttle bonnet of ancient pattern, a short skirt and men's shoes, and as she pushed her little cart through miles and miles of country lanes she composed long poems, which being too illiterate to commit to paper she, like the bards of old, learnt by heart and repeated in a singsong tone to all who cared to hear them. They were moral tales, with here and there a hint of real poetic feeling and an appreciation of the beauty of Nature, but in rhyme and rhythm they were sadly deficient.

Between these two women a strange rivalry existed, and when the basket-maker's husband died she spent £16 on erecting a huge stone to her husband's memory, the object of which was avowedly to outdo the one which the rag and bone lady had placed over *her* husband's grave years before.

The last time I saw my old friend the poet she was in a resplendent bonnet of purple silk with a very full cap border, in honour of the wedding of the last of her many foster sons. She died shortly after, and it was found that she was quite a woman of property having, if I remember rightly, about £100 laid by in the house. The discovery was a disappointing one to the many friends who had helped her substantially under the impression, which she certainly did not discourage, that when she ceased to be able to go her rounds she would be in need of assistance.

Well, peace be to their ashes. There is no rivalry in the grave where both now lie, and maybe old feuds are now made up. The basket-woman's cats have passed to other hands, and my old friend's poetry has died with her, all but one long tale in doggerel verse, written out in a childish hand by one of the children of the National School at her dictation, which *may* be still preserved, though I cannot answer for it that it is so.

She was not the only unlettered poet that Heddingden produced. Next door to my garden an old soldier and his comely hard-working wife, had bought a bit of land and erected a little shanty as small and snug as a ship's cabin. A couple of greenhouses, in which however nothing ever flourished, vied with the dwellinghouse in size, and the old man spent his life in his garden. Some strange lack in his character resulted in his never having the thing you needed. When ducks were in season his green peas were in flower. His raspberries were over before his currants were ripe. His sprouts were so late or the frosts so early that he never had any for the table, and his celery was either not earthed up soon enough or rotted in the ground before it was dug. He was up with the lark and worked on by moonlight, but had it not been for his sensible hardheaded wife he would I verily believe have ended his days in the workhouse.

But then he too was a poet, and what could one expect? His poetry took the form of parable and gave him intense pleasure. He was a great Bible reader too, and meditated much on what he read, puzzling over mystic numbers, of days and years, of 'times, and a time, and half a time.'

He went out gardening, but was as unsuccessful with other people's gardens as with his own. But his manners were courteous as became an old soldier and he had a great feeling for law and order. It was good to see his well brushed white hair and beard, decent Sunday coat and reverent aspect as he came regularly to his Communion. He was terribly deaf and generally read his Bible at home instead of coming to other services, or if there he brought with him a book of sermons to read while the vicar preached. There was something pathetic in the old man's soldierly attention to duty, together with his lack of success.

Though a hero of the Indian Mutiny, and though his three sons and his daughter were all born under the Queen's flag, he had been content to live unnoticed, and had never claimed his pension. Our clergyman on finding this applied for it, but it was only a few years ago, and it was only this year (1909) that the old man, then over eighty, was called up before his fellow parishioners at the yearly village flower show to receive his Indian Mutiny medal. He broke down into tears of joy and gratitude as it was pinned on his breast.

The old man and his wife still live to enjoy their honours. Long may they do so. I found them kind neighbours, and he never failed to take his pipe out of his mouth as he passed me, lest the smoke should blow into my face, old *gentleman* that he was.

My next door neighbours on the other side were not so pleasing.

They came, a party of eight, on a fine day when I was as usual employed in my garden. And when teatime came, knowing well the fatigue of a move and the difficulty of getting a comfortable meal,

I sent my little maid in with a tray of eight breakfast cups and saucers and a fat teapot of tea. It was received with joy, and brought back by the eldest son of the family, a young man with the face of a horse and the air of a dissenting Minister or an undertaker. In spite of the work in which he was engaged he was dressed in a black coat and waistcoat of as clerical a cut as was consistent with being a layman, and his thanks were gracious and profuse.

Thus friendlily did our acquaintance begin. The master of the house was bailiff to one of our farmers and he had a son and daughter by a former marriage, and so had she, and there were two younger children by the present marriage. He was a small frightened looking man, and she a stout buxom woman with a grand air who all too evidently ruled the roost. As he was deaf, and she had a loud tongue, their frequent quarrels were plainly to be heard through the thin walls of our jerry-built houses, and I soon discovered that they would not be agreeable neighbours. The funereal son and a pretty little sister of sixteen seemed worth cultivating, and as we were needing Sunday school teachers I suggested to our vicar the possibility of their being able and willing to help. He however had not had a very encouraging account of them from their former rector, so no steps were taken in that direction.

In the meantime I was persecuted by the visits of a pet lamb, almost the size of a full-grown sheep, which contrived to push open my gate and browse on my newly cultivated garden. I had *just* coaxed a few flowers to flourish in the unkindly soil of what had been a brickfield, and was inflated with pride that I had succeeded in training a mass of golden and brown chrysanthemums to look in at the bow window of my dining room, when the pet lamb spent a night in my garden, and when I came down to breakfast not a flower was left. I had several times entreated them to keep the lamb within their own domain, and now I spoke once more.

That I might not make a formal complaint I waited till I saw Mrs Brand in the garden and then unfolded to her my woes. She answered with asperity that it was "only a pore lamb" as if that fact would heal the wound of my flowerless condition. I told her the difficulty I had had in getting anything to grow in my neglected garden and then, lest I should seem unfriendly towards an animal that was evidently a pet, I remarked, "I suppose you have had it a long time?" She shot a glance of venom at me, and exclaiming "That's a kind of question one does not ask" flung into the house and banged the door behind her.

I was at a loss as to how the question had offended her, till I heard that the lamb was a stray one that they had annexed, and my interest in its 'birth, patronage and education' had touched upon a sore spot.

Other and worse sores however were to follow. A request that I should lend her some brandy, and a conscious giggle when on one occasion she came out into the garden with a tumbler in her hand, albeit it was empty, and the remark "I am ashamed that you should see me with this," gave me an insight into the cause of the constant quarrels and general combativeness of my stout neighbour, and except that the pretty little daughter came to me weekly for a literature class I saw very little of them.

Then the crisis came.

An awful smell of drains sent both my servant and myself to bed with sore throats and general symptoms of gastric trouble, and the situation being already strained I did not speak personally, but sent for the Inspector of Nuisances to look into the matter and kept my own drains diligently flushed. That the smell came from next door there was no doubt, it being overpowering every time one passed a certain crack in the partition wall between the two houses. The workman who came to plaster up the crack, where he stripped off the paper, described it as 'fit to knock one down'.

Well, the Inspector came, and as is usual with that intelligent kind of person he left his nose behind him, refused to discover any odour and told me to clean out my ashpit, which of course I immediately did. He at my request went next door, chummed up with my neighbours, and nothing came of the visit.

I then wrote to beg that the cesspool, which was situated in their garden, might be cleaned out, saying that of course I expected to share the expense. They promised to do it, though with a very bad grace, and still nothing was done. Once more I had to write and beg that the matter might be attended to, and this time with the result that the following epistle was dropped into my letter box.

> "Mr Langton replies for Mrs Brand and wishes to know if Miss Rivers expects she can compel people to carry out what is required. She has undertaken to fulfil the engagement and has been promised to have it done, and have been disappointed in their not coming last night and have just heard their promise to come tonight. It might have been done before if Miss Rivers had said Mrs B would you get Mr B to look at the cesspool and he would have thought to look How was he to know when it should

be full and not go and set an Inspector to work Is that your Christian spirit Is that doing justice to your neighbour. Some Surly men could have made a lot of Bother of it, but as it was he was not and we have carried out what he wished so far as we can and Mr Langton asks Miss Rivers not to make a village talk and tell an untruth into the bargain and say that Mrs Brand did not try to get it done, as she did about Miss B saying she had ask her to take a class in the Sunday school and she refused on account of duties at Home, while at the same time She, and myself were waiting for the office and had been while 2 classes at school were often put into one but of course I have lived here long enough to learn that though you have splendid qualities you are too self righteous to allow others to help in Church work you Like to tell people no one does anything in the parish but you, while you are simply barring others I never saw anything like it in any parish before trusting the men will come tonight as promised at four o'clock this afternoon

"Believe me faithfully yours

"J. Langton

"for Mr and Mrs B
"Sunny Side
"Heddingden March 29 1893"

As I had done my best to get the vicar to offer the brother and sister a class in the Sunday school, this indictment seemed rather undeserved, but they could not know this, and of course I did not fight out the point. As far as any notice being taken of the letter, it might never have been written, and I suspect considerable disappointment was felt at the fact that I returned no answer and continued to treat my neighbours with courtesy.

Not long after that they were sold up and left the place, and when the landlord came to look to repairs it was discovered that a broken drainpipe was pouring its contents into their cellar, which was connected with mine by a drain intended to counteract any damp that might rise from the ground, so that though I constantly poured buckets of Condy's fluid down my side of the drain, the bad air from their side made the house unhealthy and the smell was insupportable.

My friend of epistolary powers ended strangely. When his people departed he took lodgings in the village, and with the aid of a tutor endeavoured to pass the requisite examinations for Holy Orders. In this he failed, but a new vicar coming he was made a sort of lay reader,

Old photograph of a local farm.

and during a long illness which obliged me to resign the post he was appointed superintendent of the Sunday school.

Sticks, acorns and chestnuts were again introduced, and one saw the wisdom of the former vicar in refusing to employ him in the school.

Then a strange thing happened. He left the neighbourhood, and returned, bringing with him something very like a lady as his wife! She had been governess in a good family, was a musician and a linguist, and had a good education and good manners. How in spite of representing himself as a man of fortune he had succeeded in getting her to listen to his addresses it was difficult to imagine; but there was the fact, and bitterly did she repent her hasty act when she found him deeply in debt and in no sense her equal. Once more they were sold up and disappeared from the village, as they now do from my life.

Chapter IV

THE BOWDONS

"We must not be too sagacious in judging people by the little excrescences of their character"

The Poet at the Breakfast-Table

There seems to me a danger that those who hear my experiences will either believe that the whole population of Heddingden were lunatics, or suspect me to be insane myself, as it is well-known to be a feature of insanity to believe all the world to be mad except oneself.

There are plenty more lunatics to come! But in the meanwhile I must introduce a family whose unlikeness to the rest of the world in no way consisted of weakness or want of balance.

Mr Bowdon was the owner of a mill which did brisk work whenever the winds would set it a-going, and that was on all but very still days as it crowned the only hill in the flat land around. Heavy wagons climbed the hill and left their freight of corn which was merrily ground into 'firsts' or 'seconds' by the resounding millstones which droned like an imprisoned bumble bee and soothed me to sleep on many a windy night, when the miller worked late to grind wheat, which takes more power than barley or oats. The mill served me as a weathercock, and never till I lived in its near neighbourhood and heard the 'singing' of the flywheel as it flashed round and turned the 'bonnet' to a sudden change of wind, did I realise how often the wind can change in a single day. I found it quite a companion and missed its music on still sultry days. But on thundery *nights* it became a very weird neighbour indeed. Its dazzling white sides caught the colour of the vivid flashes of lightning, which not infrequently played on each side in turn, and vicious blue light would be followed by rose colour, green or angry white, and between the flashes darkness would swallow it and the surrounding country in inky blackness.

From the hill on which the mill stood we could count nine churches and it was a grand place for sunsets.

Old postcard of the Church and Old Vicarage, showing the spire which was later removed.

The same scene today.

Every day Mr Bowdon climbed the hill and had a chat with the miller, so that I soon got to know his grey coat and broad-brimmed felt hat. It was some time before I wedded him to his sensible and active wife, though she was very much to the fore, and I often met or passed her in the street. But she looked a typical old maid, and I could hardly believe it possible not only that she had been married for over forty years but that she had had eight or nine children. It was yet longer before I connected her with a row of little graves in the churchyard, which told the sad tale of four little ones cut off within a few weeks of each other by scarlet fever years before.

I am afraid I did not appreciate the family at first, and was more struck by Mrs Bowdon's loud voice and dictatorial manner, and her rather fussy way of doing things, than by their real worth and cleverness.

There had been Bowdons at Heddingden as far back as History went. Ninety Heddingden men had joined the Jack Cade rebellion, amongst whom a Bowdon was conspicuous. Whether he was one of those who were hanged at Tyburn I am not sure, but am inclined to think he was. Another ancestor had been one of those who sailed in the *Mayflower,* and their house and furniture spoke of solid forefathers and foremothers. Lovely old china, original copies of standard works, and quaint pieces of furniture told of Bowdons from whom it was good to be descended. And when I got to know more of them I found that china and curiosities were not their only heritage, but that they had also come in for more than the usual share of brains and business capacity.

One delicate handsome girl of fourteen was still left to them, and three sons, one of whom showed a considerable taste for drawing, and brought me along with my morning loaf some very creditable sketches of the neighbourhood.

The girl, Ella, had unfortunately been kept from school by ill health, and at first when she joined a little literature class that I started I thought her so far behind the others as to be rather a drag upon the class. She read haltingly, and wrote so slowly that I had to take notes for her. But though without school learning she soon proved herself to have more real education than any of the party.

It was she who, when I myself was at fault as to who were the 'Gubbings' mentioned in *Westward Ho,* looked them up in one of the old family books and copied out all the information we needed. It was she who, when we were reading Mallory's *Morte d'Arthur,* brought me a sketch copied by herself of the cross that marks King Arthur's grave at Glastonbury. It was she who, when *Town Geology* was the book we were reading, brought specimens of different geological strata, and an account of a great landslip, and when I took botany as our subject it was she who knew where all the rare plants were to be found, who introduced me to the great spearwort and who showed a keen interest in a knowledge of the habits and growth of plants. It was she too who, when I set them to draw the flowers we examined from nature, beat all the others both in the faithfulness of her representations and the delicacy of her touch.

I set them to draw the flowers we studied, in the hope that she might excel in that particular, as I was touched to see her struggling vainly with the spelling of the botanical names, with tears of discouragement raining down her face as she found herself left hopelessly behind the rest of the class.

Gradually one learnt to appreciate the cleverness and real worth of the father and mother, and ceased to mind the bumptiousness which gentle blood might not have eradicated but would have concealed under gentle manners.

Never was there a parish tea to be prepared for that Mrs Bowdon did not take half the trouble off the shoulders of the vicar's wife. Every sale of work saw her regular at the meetings, willing to work at home, and foremost among the decorators and saleswomen. Was anything wanted? She had it, or knew where to get it, or who would lend it. Were strawberries or raspberries needed for the tea? Their garden was stripped for the fray, and dainty plates arranged with fruit ready picked were put on the table, and all trouble saved not only to the sellers but also to the eaters.

But some Shakespeare readings started by one of our vicars (we lived to see four in succession before we left the parish) brought out other talents at which I had not even guessed. I hope and believe that it was I who turned Ella into a good reader of Shakespeare, but I was yet to learn that the loud voiced miller himself excelled in the art. He begged to have the part of 'Old Gobbo' as he, with an acumen amounting to genius, remarked that his voice and pronunciation would suit the part. I had the pleasure of reading Launcelot to his Gobbo and we played into each other's hands with mutual zest. Always he asked for some part such as the Fool or the Peasant for a character, where the play would not suffer from his Kentish twang, while his daughter read and read well such parts as Rosalind with a nice distinction between coquetry and vulgarity.

Every year Mr and Mrs Bowdon, with knapsacks on their backs, went a walking tour, and I do not think I am exaggerating when I say that they knew every cathedral and most buildings of any note in England. And no flower or geological curiosity that came their way was neglected. It was difficult to hear without smiling his confident assertion that he had in a few months, and unaided, 'learnt French', that he might travel abroad, for his English was so very provincial that it required a stretch of imagination to conceive what his French would be like. Anyway he went to France, saw a good deal and enjoyed himself there. His self confidence doubtless helped him to make himself understood where a more modest or shyer man would have been floored.

Kind souls! I get a great welcome from them both when I return to my old home, and Mr Bowdon never ceases to tell me how much he appreciates and values five big volumes of Hone with which I presented him on my departure. They would be I knew quite after his own heart, and they were not after mine, so he was the gainer and I not the loser. So his great gratitude makes me feel rather ashamed of the transaction though it is a pleasure to feel that they have given him real pleasure.

Some little time before we left the village was electrified by the appearance of a very smart family in a very smart motor car, who stopped at the Bowdons' house. We heard with considerable interest that the descendant of the 'Mayflower Bowdon' had come to England and to Heddingden to make acquaintance with his English relations. His greeting to our Mr Bowdon was quaint and original. "So after three hundred years we meet again." The American Bowdons had kept to the ancient spelling of the family name and were great people in their adopted country, as appeared when it was discovered that he was one of the invited guests at some great function at the White House. Who then so proud as his English cousins to welcome him to the mother country, and who so proud as he to claim kindred with his English relations, or to tread once more the soil from which his ancestors sprang, as the dwellers in that brand new country.

They stayed several days with the old miller, and when they left it was with the promise of returning to celebrate their daughter's wedding in the old country and in the old church of Heddingden.

Great was the festivity at the wedding of the millionaire's daughter, but we were not there to see it and were only able to hear and read the brilliant accounts of it.

Two tangible results followed. A brass let into the chantry floor at the foot of the side altar, in memory of the original Bowdon from whom both families sprang, and a very good painted window in the north wall of the nave, in remembrance of the wedding.

There remains a hope in the minds of their Heddingden relations that yet another memorial may be erected to a certain Robina Bowdon who plays rather a conspicuous part in the family archives, though what form it is likely to take no one knows. A new organ I believe is the suggestion of the English relations. I confess that the completion of the rood screen lies nearer my heart. That it should be so beautifully begun, and fail of completion, would be very sad, and the organ is sure to come some day. That appeals to everyone, but what is the use of reckoning our chickens before they are hatched, especially American chickens in an English home.

Chapter V

HAROLD CROWDER ESQUIRE

"He fondly imagines . . . that he is but an ordinary individual, exciting no unusual interest; a nonentity as far as his neighbours are concerned – and therefore takes little pains to conceal his movements and his opinions"

Alfred W. Rees

During the whole of the first part of our life at Heddingden my sister not only played the organ, trained the choir and had a Bible class for boys, but also carried on her orphanage, that is to say clothed, fed and educated a dozen boys on five shillings a week each, though I fear she often went short herself to give them advantages they would never have had in other Homes. I have known the time when she was so short of money that she had to borrow of the boys themselves the pennies to get their hair cut by the village barber. Why the pennies were needed I do not know, for in the general way she cut all their hair herself, and not only acted barber but also tailor to the whole family.

She begged cast off clothes from her gentlemen friends, put them through the washing machine and turned out her boys in Eton jackets, the only garment into which a gentleman's dress coat can be made. So well were they made, and so smart did the boys look in their Eton collars, that strangers generally spoke of them as "the young gentlemen".

She had the most capable hands I ever saw, and could win the race at needlework with the quickest needlewoman of my acquaintance. Indeed she was one of the most 'all round' clever people I have known, with brain as well as hands.

In her long years of managing an orphanage she was sure as may be supposed to come across strange stories and odd characters. I wish she had written down her experiences at the time, for I have to piece

Juliana Poole, Aunt Penelope's elder sister, Aunt Joanna.

together from memory some of the sad or curious stories after the lapse of years. But no notice of Heddingden at that date would be complete without some account of her work, and I may add of *herself* and the curious lives and characters of some of the boys who lived with her.

Of these stories one of the saddest was that of a child sent to her by the Society for the Prevention of Cruelty to Children*, who had been kept for three years in a room by himself, where his food – scraps such as you would give to a dog – was pushed under the door and eaten how and when he could get it. When first discovered by the Society he was in a filthy and emaciated condition and had worn a hole in the floor by the door by constantly standing there, and in the panels of the door itself by kicking them in the endeavour to get out.

When brought to her he was a bonny sturdy-looking child, with a handsome face and beautiful eyes, but his temper was so spoilt by the ill treatment to which he had been subjected that it was impossible for anyone but a man to manage him. He was soon handed on to the Gordon Home where he throve and prospered exceedingly, turning out a fine happy lad, repaying well those who trained him.

Among other odd characters was a boy of ten, Harold Crowder by name. A strong thickset child with a sort of rather coarse handsomeness of his own, and a pair of brown velvet eyes. He was not a

*Founded in 1884, became the N.S.P.C.C. in 1889.

pleasant child, would make anyone whom he was strong enough to coerce do his work, and he was boastful and hectoring in tone and manner. He had a loud and not very musical voice and a good ear, so that he soon took a part in the choir with ease. But he had to be constantly checked for drowning all the other parts with his stentorian voice.

On one such occasion he flung out of the room in a towering rage and shouted, "The fact is you're jealous of me, you can't sing a bit yourself, and as to Miss Penelope she screams like a cat". As it happens my sister had a peculiarly sweet voice and understood music both in theory and practice. His temper was overbearing to his equals, and to his elders he displayed a strange mixture of passion and sullenness very difficult to deal with.

My sister did not like him, nor he her, and I am bound to say that after knowledge showed that she had not understood him. He gave himself great airs, and among the many little things that annoyed her he scrawled all over the door "H. Crowder *Esqre*". If he might not take the lead in anything he would not do the thing at all, and refused to play second fiddle not only figuratively but literally to a boy a little older than himself who was further advanced on the violin than he. He never attended to his work, and if told that he had forgotten or neglected anything he cocked his chin in the air and said he was "composing".

And all this while the boy was really growing his wings, and rubbing his shoulders with irritation in the process as most folks of genius do.

He left my sister, with no regret on either side, and would probably have remained misunderstood and unappreciated to the end had not the same indefatigable friend who had stood by the Dudleys in their trouble taken him up. She got him into the band of a crack regiment, gave him private lessons with a first rate master, and H. Crowder *Esqre.* is now really a musician and composer whose compositions are played in the Albert Hall. His music is so appreciated that he is always being asked as a solo violinist to play at grand houses and to take part in first rate concerts.

I have just heard that he has married, his bride having gone out to join him in India. The wife of the Colonel of the Regiment offered to chaperone the bride and take her into her own house for the night before the wedding, but Harold had already made arrangements with the sergeant major's wife to receive and take care of her. So the Colonel's wife lent her carriage to take the guests to and from the church.

The school and schoolhouse as they were in Joanna's time and as they are today. There are no visible changes other than the removal of the bell tower.

Poor lad, he is a professed atheist now, and is as proud of his atheism as he was of his musical powers in the days of old. He is steady, saving, and apparently moral in his conduct, but it is an unpleasing character. Even the lady who has befriended him for so many years, and who has had the pleasure of seeing the fruits of her kindness, feels more interest in his career than affection for himself. Perhaps marriage will do great things for him, but unless his wife has stirred his affections, *heart* seems left out of his composition. A hard and cold sense of duty seems to be keeping him straight. What will be the end of such a character?

So many of my sister's boys were sent to her by the Society for the Prevention of Cruelty to Children that it did not at all follow that their parents were dead, and an Irish reply given by one of them when asked "And who are you?" was not so strange as it was amusing. "Please sir, I'm one of Miss Rivers's orphans and my father and mother live in London." Of course some of these, though by no means all, came from the slums, but on the whole the boys were bona fide orphans and came of respectable parents. But whatever their antecedents, most of them turned out well in character and rose in the social scale.

To one indeed came a curious piece of good fortune. He was a clerk in a London firm, and a Russian nobleman to whom he was teaching English adopted him, and the last time I saw him the slim refined boy had turned into a gentlemanly young man who did not look out of place as a nobleman's son. Several went to the colonies and one clever boy became head of a large school in South Africa, whither he went after the Boer War.

It was pleasant to see my sister with her stalwart 'sons' when they returned, as they often did, to the old Home for their holidays. With them came others whom she had taught long before the orphanage had been started or even thought of. Among them was a canon of the Cathedral of Bridgetown, Barbados, who had married a friend of the Bishop. He was the son of a small farmer in my father's parish and went out as a missionary from St Augustine's College. Another is an actor in a wellknown touring company and a third is headmaster of a cathedral school in Scotland.* From another schoolmaster I had a visit last summer (1911). He found himself six miles from our new home and had walked over to see his old friend's grave.

*See note at end of chapter

Of her many grownup orphans one continued to live with her, and Heddingden must have gasped with amazement when they found that her house was shared by a young carpenter who spent his evenings with her and was treated as an equal.

Whether the arrangement was a wise one for either party there may be two opinions, and many people gave a half pitying smile at its unconventionality. It was certainly odd, and as I write the word I am reminded of my niece's remark about the Heddingden oddities: "You and Aunt Joanna will head the list!" I had forgotten it, but I am bound to confess that I think 'Aunt Joanna' would make a very good story if I could get far enough off to see her from an outsider's point of view. Perhaps some day when I am gone, our niece may really tell the tale. She was fond of her, and could throw just that veil of tenderness and humour over it which would be needed to make it an appreciation as well as an amusing story.

Note:

Since writing this I have had a great pleasure.

A visit to the north of England gave me a longing to cross the border and see the master of the cathedral school before mentioned, and also his wife who was an old scholar of mine. Each had been one of the best loved of many well loved pupils, and it was with great interest that my sister and I had watched their growing attachment, which began when they were but boy and girl.

If my tale were not of Heddingden my old scholar might have found a place in it as her circumstances were peculiar.

I first made her acquaintance when, as a child of nine, I found her sitting forlornly on a bench in the Infant School with the tiny tots of four or five, learning her letters. Born on a coal barge, her father had just taken a small public house in the village, and in these unpromising surroundings she developed into a singularly modest and intelligent girl. As she grew up she became my right hand in everything, and finally married our young schoolmaster.

I grow garrulous in my old age and long to tell of their wedding on a certain Ascension Day, of how the wedding party gathered together for the early Celebration, teachers and scholars kneeling side by side at the altar before the marriage service. But the story belongs to another parish and a different epoch in our lives. Suffice it to say that they crowned an early attachment with a happy married life and eventually settled in Scotland, and there in their own house after twenty-four years I spent a delightful week with them.

It was a week that might well fill my cup of thankfulness to the brim as I saw them surrounded by their four bonny daughters, who treated their parents with that mixture of petting and deference which tells of perfect love and understanding. The girls were what a friend of mine would call 'a job lot', so unlike were they to each other both in character and appearance. But I came away from that happy God-fearing household glad at heart, for all that we had longed for for our two 'children', as we had loved to call them, was being lived out in their lives, and in the lives of their children after them.

We steamed down the Caledonian Canal together, they and I on my homeward journey, as far as Fort Augustus, and my last sight of them was as they stood waving farewell as the boat followed the curve of the lake and the wooded banks, golden with gorse and broom in the June sunshine, hid them from my sight.

I have stayed in many houses, rich and poor, but in none have I had a warmer welcome or a kinder host and hostess.

My only regret is that my sister never had the pleasure of sharing their hospitality. (June 1912)

Penelope Rivers, Ellen M. Poole, in her garden.

Chapter VI

SAMUEL HOMEWOOD

"Oh, a body could both cry and laugh"

Peer Gynt p. 57

"It will always be a comfort to me", remarked Miss Jeffrey dreamily, "to feel that whatever happens, I haven't been absolutely overlooked. I may not have got married but no one can say I haven't been took notice of."

Mrs Galer's Business

It was soon after we settled in Heddingden that I noticed a young man in church whose regularity and behaviour singled him out as one who had been brought up in habits at least of reverence and order, probably of devotion.

'Groom' was writ large all over him from the closecut hair to the slightly bandy legs, yet his dress, though well brushed and put on with a certain air of smartness inseparable from his class, was very poor, and his pallid complexion and spare frame gave one the impression that he was ill fed.

After noticing him for several Sundays, and vainly enquiring whether anyone could tell me anything about him, I found him one day in the churchyard moving some very heavy slabs of stone with neither rollers nor a friendly hand to help him. One could see the play of the muscles of back and arms through the thin shirt, and it seemed to me only too likely that he would strain himself seriously in the endeavour to do by himself the work of two, so I stopped and spoke to him.

"That's heavy work", I said, "Can you not borrow rollers to help you in it?"

He stopped a moment to touch his cap and answer my question, and then with no desire apparently for further conversation he tried again to raise the block on which he was engaged. Knowing that my

No 1985 photograph could show this view taken from Penelope's gate. The Church still dominates the scene, but a high dense hedge now borders the road and many new houses have been built behind it.

sister had rollers, and would willingly send a boy or two to help, I left him, saying I would send a couple of boys and some rollers. And again, with a mere touch of the hat and a "Thank you, ma'am", and no attempt either to grumble over the work or to ingratiate himself with me, I left him.

The post office was kept by one of the churchwardens, and of him I enquired what he could tell me about my new friend.

"He seems down on his luck, so I gave him the job", said the churchwarden. "I believe he's lodging at the Unicorn and I really believe the poor fellow's half pined. He seems a respectable fellow too, and strong and willing and very glad of the job."

I had inherited from the last tenants of my house, as I think I have already said, a garden that needed entire making and a considerable expenditure of strength in the doing of it, and having *very* limited means and not a superabundance of time to spare I had had serious thoughts of letting the ground to some labourer for a cabbage patch. But it would have broken my heart to have done so. Now a new notion came into my head. What if I could give this poor fellow work for a few weeks until he had got something in the way of a situation?

When my sister set up the school for tradesmen's children, of which I have spoken, three sisters of our clergyman, Lawrence by name, shared in the work, each coming for a quarter to teach in the school and board with me. They were exceedingly nice girls. They were capable, energetic, very kind-hearted, putting their whole soul into parish and school work, and – after all not a thing to be despised – each possessing a little money of her own, with which in a truly liberal spirit they helped their brother in his parish needs.

When I got home I told Emily Lawrence of my interview with the young man in the churchyard, and of my thought as to whether I could manage to screw out enough money to give him a few weeks' work.

I cannot say that I was surprised, though I was much delighted, by her at once offering to find the money if I would find the work. This was soon settled, and Samuel Homewood was installed as gardener under me. There had never been a time when I was not an enthusiastic gardener and now, instead of having to use my little plot of ground to rear another man's cabbages, I had the pleasure of seeing it grow into a garden by our united efforts.

Never did man work with more goodwill and energy, though his knowledge of gardening was of the smallest. He hissed as he 'rubbed down' the plants, cleaned the butts, swept out the yard, chopped pea sticks or riddled soil, or did any of the many jobs for which a man's hand was desirable. His great pride and delight was a bit of lawn which he made entirely himself, levelling the ground, cutting the turf and laying it with his own hands. Every day he planned and worked, and put in young greens or chopped firewood, and one could *see* him growing in self respect and happiness in every look and movement.

I saw a great deal of him, for I gave myself up very much to my garden while I had a strong hand to aid me. Besides that he came regularly to my men's Bible class and hovered about doing any little thing he could for me, both in house and garden. Yet for all that he remained a bit of an enigma.

He spoke of having had good parents both of whom were dead, and a brother of whom he had lost sight. His mother had been somewhere (was it a hospital or a lunatic asylum?) where he visited her once a year. But he never told me where the place was or why she was there. There was a hiatus too in his own life. He told me of his school days, of his Confirmation, of a place where he had been groom-gardener for seven years, and of one or two situations which he had kept for short periods; of his pleasure in long Sunday walks to the different churches in the neighbourhood and of their services and

The Workhouse, originally a clothworkers' hall, sketched by Louis Wain.

their preachers, but especially of their styles of architecture. He was most anxious that I should see some of them and would describe their architectural features in glowing terms. His knowledge had been gleaned from some papers in the local newspaper and absorbed with avidity.

He was very emotional, spoke with tears of his parents, and I once caught him watching a funeral as it passed my gate. He brushed his hand across his eyes as he turned away, and then he spoke of his own death. He had once nearly drowned and felt a great desire for life, and then somehow our talk drifted on to the subject of Holy Communion. He had been confirmed but wished it was to come all over again. He had thought little of it at the time; he was with a careless set, and he was as careless as the rest. No, he was not a Communicant, he had never come as he had felt afraid.

Then began daily readings with me in the evenings to help him to prepare for his first Communion and they made a good excuse for keeping him to supper. Though he was awed, interested, and sometimes opened out a good deal on other points, there was a dead wall against which I was brought up short and there were a certain three years of which he could, or would, give no account.

All this time I was moving Heaven and Earth to get him a place, speaking for him, writing for him, answering advertisements and begging clothes from my gentlemen friends so that I might send him out well clad. I had a right therefore to enquire into what his life had been, and several times said, "But, Homewood, there are three years of which you have given me no account. Where were you then?" And each time a curious vague look came into his face which made me wonder whether his mother had indeed been a lunatic, and he too had failed mentally, and really could not recall the events of those years.

He gave the names of two of his former masters to whom I wrote, asking if they would be good enough to give him a character. One refused, stating no reason for doing so, but as it was four or five years since he had been with him, that might account for it. The other spoke well of him, but said he had been there but a short time – only a few months. And armed with this letter I got him a situation.

He had worked for me for three months and had shown both zeal and affection, but though doing exactly what he was told, neat-handedly, he struck me as wanting in initiative, and a something – I can hardly tell what – made me sometimes wonder whether he drank. Perhaps it was partly his pasty complexion, white lips and red-rimmed eyes, or perhaps it was the occasional vagueness of manner of which I have spoken. I made enquiries of my Bible class men and they all said he was sober. They thought him 'odd' and rather 'scared', but he was 'all right' they added.

Privately a thought occurred to me. Did he take opium? I knew it was sold at the Unicorn where he lodged, but I had no right to put a mere surmise into other heads than my own, and I heard no gossip that could in any way lead me to believe that it was so.

When I paid him his last wages, and saw him in his groom's suit of clothes, I said, "And now, Homewood, I can't afford a shilling more. You are well started and I hope to hear good things of you".

So the next day I set to work on my garden without my faithful friend, but as I was turning to wheel a heavy barrow of earth a voice

This postcard of the Old Workhouse is a little more recent, though nevertheless of the time of Penelope Rivers. It shows a new door at the near end of the building and a way into Church Walk from the main road.

at my side said, "I don't like to see you doing that, ma'am", and there he was, leaning over the fence and looking at me with longing eyes.

He made several more remarks and at last, seeing that he was wishing to help but was too shy to offer to do so I said, "I think I know what you want to say. I can't afford to give you a job, but if you care to come in and help me for love I shall be pleased to accept it". So in he came, and worked quite as hard for love as he had done for money.

He cleaned out my cellar too, and when he was gone I found that he had contrived to rig up two or three shelves out of some spare wood that he thought would be convenient for me to store my bulbs on.

Well, we knelt side by side at the altar on the next Sunday and then he went, first carrying down my bag to the station and seeing me off for my summer holiday. The last sight I had of him was as he turned away, a suspicious mist in his eyes as he watched the receding train, and his last words as we grasped hands out of the carriage window were "You've been a mother to me".

So with many hopes and almost more fears I left him with a promise on both sides that we would write.

He wrote often and fully, telling me exactly what his work was. He spoke of being comfortable and getting on well, and two or three times the carrier left at my door a large and beautiful cucumber, 'a gift from Homewood'.

A characteristic note accompanied it. "The gardener tells me that if I don't have them they will only go to the pigs, so I am his 'pig' while they last." He described the church and its services, and sounded happy and interested in his work.

Then one day, when he had been just three months in his place, I saw his wellknown figure pass the window, and a sudden presentiment of evil filled my mind. He came in very hot and very indignant; he had been turned off. He seemed at a loss to know why. It appeared that he had turned the carriage clumsily in coming out of the yard and had scratched the paint, and his master had discharged him at once. An angry letter from his master followed, saying he was lazy and had once fallen asleep during family prayers. Then I remembered that I had on one occasion found him asleep in the wheelbarrow when he was working for me.

What could be done? Nothing. It was with difficulty that I had got him a character and a fresh start, and now I could do no more. We talked it over sorrowfully, and I found that the only relation he had any dealings with was in one of the big towns in the Midlands. He was absolutely thrown on his own resources again and they were small. Could he get a post as cab driver in the town where his aunt lived? It seemed doubtful, especially as he confessed that his nerve was gone. But it appeared the best chance we could think of.

I wrote to a cousin of my own who was walking the hospital there, and asked him to look after him and be good to him. Then once more, still less hopefully this time, I saw him depart.

My cousin asked him to tea in his lodgings and took him for a walk in the country, and by and by I found he was driving a cab. Again he wrote to me pretty regularly.

Then quite suddenly his letters ceased, and I was beginning to be uneasy about him, when I was surprised by a visit from an Inspector of Police who came to ask what I knew of him. He was in gaol on a charge of robbing the alms box of a church. When arrested he refused to give either name or address, but a letter from me was found in his pocket. So they came to me to give what account I could of him.

That he who took such intelligent interest in architecture and joined so regularly in the services of the church should really be

The Old Workhouse in 1985 showing how little the building has altered. It is now used for commercial purposes and is known as The Cloth Hall.

guilty of robbing an alms box seemed to me well nigh impossible. That being found haunting churches for no ostensible reason should have led to his arrest seemed not improbable. Of course I told the Inspector all I knew and spoke of Homewood's faithful work for me, and I wrote to the chaplain of the gaol about him. Unfortunately the chaplain was away, and when he returned Homewood had just been released, so the letter I had enclosed for him never reached him. I lost sight of him. I could get no clue as to his whereabouts and he was doubtless ashamed to make the first move.

A couple of years or so later I was staying with friends at Chester. We had taken one of the little river steamers to a favourite landing place when, talking to a member of the band who 'made music' as we sailed, a face so like Homewood's struck my eye that I made a step forward with the intention of claiming acquaintance. But the look that met my eye seemed to have so little of recognition in it that I came to the conclusion that I had made a mistake, and I drew back. Years after I found that it had indeed been he, and I have never ceased to regret that I allowed myself to be so easily turned from my purpose. The very fact that I half came forward, and then drew back, may have made him think that I recognised him but would not speak.

It would be six or seven years after this chance encounter that on taking up a newspaper my eye fell on a paragraph in which his name occurred, again as having been apprehended for robbing a church. This time he was in the prison of a town a few miles from the house in which I was staying.

I need scarcely say that I went over and asked to see the governor of the gaol, in the hope that I might be allowed to visit the poor fellow. The governor did not recommend it, saying it would be painful to me – as if I did not know that – and probably would do more harm than good as our interview would have to be in the presence of the gaoler.

I told him of my former suspicions of the opium habit and he promised to speak to the doctor about it and to give me his opinion. At the same time he warned me that it was a bad case. The man had been in and out of prison constantly. It seemed one of those cases of complete loss of self respect, together with a character too weak to regain it.

As I was not allowed to see him I contented myself with writing to him, and arranging with the chaplain of the Prisongate Mission to meet him on his being set at liberty, give him a good breakfast at my expense, and hand him on to the Church Army at whatever place seemed most suitable. Then, writing to the Church Army workshops, I promised to help in the way of money if they could provide him with work.

The letter he wrote on receiving mine in the prison did not please me. He spoke of being well fed and doing well, and the tone was rollicking and free and easy. He told me he would soon be at liberty, and spoke as if misfortune rather than his own fault had brought him there.

The chaplain met him at the prison gate as arranged, found he had thirty shillings in his pocket and so was not in need of immediate help, and passed him on to the Church Army workshops. But from them I had a very unpromising account. He did not turn up till a week after his release, and then was so tipsy as to be useless. After a time he applied again when he was sober, but he was apparently incapable of doing better work than that of sandwich man. Then he once more disappeared.

He wrote and asked me for money and I replied that I would not *give* him a farthing, but that I would provide all I could possibly afford to start him in regular work. Once more I heard of him. He wrote to ask if he might come and see me, and I invited him to tea, but waited for him in vain. Afterwards I learned that *on his way to see me* he had entered a small eating house where he tried to make off with a watch and chain, and he was once more sent to prison. Then another church was robbed; some of the money was marked, and a man was hidden in the vestry who caught him in the act, and once more he was arrested.

I got into the habit of looking at the Police reports in the daily paper, but years went by and I was thankful not to come upon his name. But where he was, or what he was doing, of that I knew nothing.

And then at last came news of him. I had been thinking more of him than usual one Sunday at the Celebration, and had been wishing that I could hear of him, and on Monday morning a letter lay on my breakfast table. With a passing wonder as to who the writer could be I opened it.

It read:

"My dear Friend" (his old form of address),

"Will you please excuse me taking the liberty of addressing you in the fase of your last. I am writing to ask you if you will marrie me. I suppose you will say it is your money that is the attraction. nothing of the kind. I have been very much in love with you from when I first knew you. I am staying here (name of place and street) till Satuarday.

Yrs very sincerely
Saml. Homewood"

It was eighteen or twenty years since we had met and I was just sixty-five. Could anything be imagined more grotesque? And yet it was pathetic too. For knowing him as I do I really believe that it was sincere, and no one can regard it as anything but a quite straightforward letter – short, with no protestations, and in a sense manly. But it was absolutely insane. Had I had any doubts of his mental condition before, I had none now, and as I pondered over the letter the position grew more and more difficult in my thoughts.

What sort of an answer could I give? Not too sympathetic or he would certainly come and call. Nor yet one to anger him if it could be helped, and in any case I felt no inclination to write such a letter. It is bad to rouse the anger of a lunatic. How had he got my address? I could not think, for I had left Heddingden three years before, and I did not know to whom he could apply unless indeed he had come over to my old home and so got my address.

The upper storey of the Old Workhouse in 1911, a pencil drawing by Ellen M. Poole, Penelope Rivers.

Well, the first thing I did was to tell my maid that it was possible that a man might come and ask for me, a man to whom years ago I had given money. I knew he was in the neighbourhood and did not intend to help him again, that if such a man appeared giving the name of Homewood I would not see him, and any man asking to see me and refusing to give a name was not to be admitted. I then wrote these few words.

"Miss P. Rivers to S. Homewood,

"What you ask is impossible. You must never either think or speak of it again."

It made my heart ache as I wrote it, for had I not been thinking of him and wanting to hear from him only the day before? How much may my thought of him have had unconscious influence upon a character highly strung, weak, and as emotional as his?

It was a hard thing to say but I must think of him no more. I must just do as did that Wise King of old, who when he had received a letter hard to answer spread it before the Lord, and asked Him to do all that could be done for the poor fellow's good, and then sternly put *all* thought of him out of my mind – even prayer, lest I should unconsciously make life harder for him.

After all could I not trust him to Higher Hands than mine, and to One whose intercessions could do naught but good?

The Old Vicarage, now Headcorn Manor. A hundred years has seen little change in this fifteenth century Wealden hall house, save that clearly the untidy tumble-down appearance of the last century has now given way to a house of great beauty.

Chapter VII

MY LADY'S BOWER

"A-most fools is outside o' Kent"

Long Will by Florence Converse

"Will said it was no use talking because his mind was made up. That he was a true Kentishman, and a British bulldog. Holdfast was his name: when he made up his mind that he was going to get anything, that thing he would have."

Chaplain of the Fleet

Among other of our beautiful black and white houses is the Old Vicarage, which stands in a corner of the churchyard and is beloved of the artists who not infrequently make our village their abode for the summer. Its oak beams, sloping roof, lattice windows, nail-studded door and vine clad walls make it well worthy of pencil and brush, especially the latter as the tiles have turned a soft plummy-purple. The vine leaves glisten claret and bronze in the sunshine, and tall orange or white lilies and the strong fronds of the male fern nod in at the lower windows.

The heavy oak door opens on to an uneven stone-flagged passage, on the left of which is the living room. Through the opposite door, generally left open as with all cottage doors, can be seen clothes blowing on the line, the cow, and an old brown donkey feeding under the apple trees, while fowls of various persuasions scratch about among the tumbledown outbuildings.

A twisted rickety staircase leads into large upper rooms with uneven floors which give one the sensation of the deck of a vessel in a storm. Yet though the house is now divided into two cottages it still bears the stamp of aristocracy, and one has but to carry one's mind back a hundred years or so to see that it must have been a dwelling of some pretention and of solid worth. Now its walls lean in the last stage of decrepitude and the sparse furniture of a cottage seems lost in the wide desert of the bare whitewashed bedrooms.

There is one room in the house however which gives a unique idea of the family who inhabit it. It is a narrow slit of a place on the right of the entrance, which when I first saw it was used and evidently meant for a dairy. A deep shelf ran round two sides of the room. The floor, which was of stone, was uncarpeted, and the whitewashed walls, albeit rickety and blistered with age, were clean and sweet. There one of the daughters of the house, her sleeves rolled up above her elbow, skimmed her pans and made up her butter with the window open to the nodding lilies. But the cow died, and with several other misfortunes coming together another was not attainable, and the dairy *as* a dairy was no more.

Most labouring families would have used the place as a lumber room, and being on the ground floor would probably have stored their potatoes in it, together with old boxes and garden tools. Not so the Freeds. One day when I went to see them Rosamond, the eldest daughter, who had been one of my best girls in the Sunday school, welcomed me with "I must show you Alma's and my room" and there it stood transmogrified.

The wide shelf, erst the abode of pans of cream, was draped with a bright valence of chintz and filled with photographs, knick-knacks and flowers in pots and vases. A carved cupboard, the work of the father, filled one corner. A teatray and a pair of bellows, carved by the two girls, were disposed against the walls, and a cabinet with shelves, made with old-fashioned mahogany bedposts and the shelves edged with an openwork railing of cotton reels placed one on another and stained to the colour of the posts, held books, china and little ornaments. A pretty paper, coloured pictures and dainty curtains to the little window had transformed it into 'My Lady's Bower'.

What other family in their position would have thought of thus beautifying the meagre little room, or of utilising the reels of which their work as village dressmakers gave them an unusual supply, in this fashion?

I know that horrified hands will be held up at the bad taste of mixing cotton reels and old fluted mahogany. Let those laugh that list; I at least could give wholehearted admiration to the inventive brains and deft fingers that had wrought this transformation, and could but add some little piece of pottery or favourite picture to the Bower. And rejoice that one was allowed to enter into the pleasure that the two girls had had in planning and executing a work that had

A little artist's licence may have been used by Louis Wain in this sketch of Headcorn Church, dating from the same time as the old post card on page 54.

given them so many happy hours, and share in the joy they felt in being able to ask their own special friends to tea in their own special room.

Their father had been a higgler* in his youth and was now an 'odd job man' with no regular situation; the mother was a plain working woman. The daughters made servants' dresses and the boys were errand boys at the little shops in the village. They were not a bit above the ordinary day labourer in position, save in turning to account every scrap of ribbon, velvet or lace, every empty reel or broken pot, and in the originality of their ideas and the industry of their fingers.

Yet these gifts enabled them not only to make their own rooms pretty and quaint, but to give pleasure to many who were poorer than themselves.

Year after year the whole family of father, mother and boys as well as girls, furnished a Christmas tree for a large and needy family with their own hands. Scraps of tinsel from last year's crackers were saved to make a fairy's wings, or to cover Liebig** pots filled with sweets. Dolls were dressed and bags, needlebooks, pincushions were made. Boxes were turned into dolls' cradles trimmed with muslin, and carts with the invariable cotton reels for wheels. The tree was supplied anonymously and these kind souls tramped up to a cottage a mile or more away after the children were in bed, to dress the tree and act Santa Claus. One year, when that particular family had left the parish and they had adopted a new one for their Christmas treat,

* an itinerant dealer
** a concentrated extract of beef

they contrived a huge snowball of cotton wool, filled it with presents and rolled it to their neighbours' door before it was light.

When grandchildren came, and they came often, and were delicate wailing little people over whom all watched with loving care, the row of stockings, one more every Christmas, were duly filled to overflowing by St Nicholas. Yet they still found time among their private charities and household kindnesses to gather berries, dry honesty seeds* and winter cherries, and get moss from the woods to decorate their own special little bit of the church – and amongst it all not to neglect their dressmaking.

An elder daughter was my servant for three years, and during that time a poor woman, whose relations lived in our parish, was burnt to death leaving five little motherless children. I appealed to my maid with the certainty that she would give willing help, we set our sewing machines to work and got five little frocks, hats and jackets ready for the poor little children in time for the funeral, she cheerfully sitting up till twelve o'clock the night before to help me to finish them.

Time was, when Freeds' own children were little, when this very girl, then only ten years old, stood on a chair to wash and iron for her mother who was ill in bed, nursed the new-born baby and took care of the other little brothers and sisters.

Mrs Freed was one of the very few cottage mothers whom I have known who kept her children rigidly from the street; and though in those days they lived in a very small cottage with almost no garden, found employment and amusement for them when indoors by cutting out pictures, making scrapbooks, dressing dolls, and using all the little odds and ends that came her way to turn into home-made toys.

Like most people with a superabundance of character the Freeds were a little 'difficult'. Take them by the right handle and they would do anything for you, but woe to the unfortunate wight who took them by the wrong one. They had the faults of their virtues, as who has not? Their self respect was liable to degenerate into pride, their firmness into obstinacy, their self reliance into opinionativeness, their love of helping their neighbours into love of influence – and they must do things their own way or not at all.

At one time I had Freed to work for me. I was laying down a path and, having had it dug two feet deep, had filled the bottom of the trench with all the old kettles and pans I could beg, borrow or steal

* known in Kent as 'money in both purses'

for drainage. Shingle, or beach as it is called in this neighbourhood, followed, and gravel was to be rolled down on the top. But with this he insisted on mixing wet clay though expressly told that whatever the result I would not have it done.

Alas! I was out in the village a few hours after, and when I came back the deed was done and I never had a dry path to the end of the chapter. I had to give up employing him as he would insist on going his own way though I laboriously impressed upon him that the garden was mine and not his.

One fatal day he was made parish clerk, and from that time he considered himself so big a man that there was no holding him and he was always at loggerheads with the vicar. Unfortunately the position of parish clerk is a freehold, and with the freehold goes, in our parish, a nice little bit of ground, the possession of which gave him both in his own eyes and in those of the village an importance which made him quite unbearable. His manners, never of the courtliest, suffered terribly.

He was devoted to the vicar, who had raised him to this dignity, though even he suffered from his obstinacy. But when others came in succession, and we have had four since we came to the parish, he was quite impossible. Nothing was right, and he took it upon himself to say when his clergyman was to bow, in what position he was to celebrate, and when and where the processional cross was to be used.

His good and really devout wife followed in his wake, and after being one of the best churchwomen in the place announced her intention of never entering the church when the cross was used. "It no ought to be there", she said emphatically, though when asked why she had no reason to offer for her assertion. And when our good vicar bowed at the words which, in the Nicene Creed, speak of Christ's Incarnation, she remarked querulously, "He no ought to bow to the Virgin"!

The enthusiasm which had made them earnest church workers had turned to gall and bitterness, and one could easily see how the spirit of fanaticism and persecution might develop out of zeal turned sour.

It was especially disappointing in their case as the vicar, whom he upheld so vigorously, had introduced most of these customs himself and held them unassailed, the pent up wrath of the 'man of Kent' being poured on the devoted head of as good a man as his predecessor – simply because he was new to the parish, and his clerk wanted to assert the dignity of his own position by bullying the parson.

For a time all the family except Rosamond turned nasty, and it was sad to see the expression on their faces change and to hear the ring of hardness that crept into their voices.

A great grief had come upon them. With the idea of converting a young man of known bad habits they had asked him to their house, introduced him to their girls and allowed the eldest daughter to become engaged to him. The sad but almost inevitable consequence followed, and mixed with deep grief and shame was the knowledge that they had fallen in the eyes of the world.

They were humiliated rather than humbled, and for the time being it seemed to shake the very foundations of their faith in their neighbours, their clergyman, their church and their God. Freed's voice grew rasping and irritable and the cause was not far to seek – he had taken to drink. I do not think he often drank till he was drunk, but he was constantly 'nipping', and though seldom or never actually drunk he was seldom quite sober either, and had always had enough to spoil his temper and make him bullying and cantankerous.

Yet under this hard exterior there was still a soft place to be found in all their hearts, the delicate child of that disastrous marriage crept into their affections, and when the old donkey was one morning discovered dead in the field, having succumbed to extreme old age, there was not a dry eye in the house.

Then illness came and one misfortune followed another. The vicar, whom they had withstood so bitterly, proved to be their best friend, and when I last saw them a gentler spirit pervaded the house. The calm faced Rosamond and the excitable Alma learnt wholesome lessons as they waited on their rapidly ageing mother who, like the man in the Bible, was 'sick of the palsy', brought on I believe by sorrow and disappointment in those she loved best. And as sorrow after sorrow fell – for sorrow has commonly a less hardening effect than disappointment – they gradually returned to their allegiance, the softer look came back to their eyes, and even the self-opinionated father was less loud and pugnacious than of old. Time, and the chastening influences of life, will surely do the rest for people who at heart are earnest and conscientious and who have a deep well of unselfish affection somewhere about them, even if for a time it has got hidden under a crust of pride and hardness.

In the palmy days of old, when the Freeds were the first to throw themselves into whatever was done for the good of the parish, they were very keen on the temperance question, and Mrs Freed came to me to know whether I would write a play on the subject for them to act. A play was not in my line, nor had I been capable of writing would they have been capable of acting one. But I planned instead a succession of tableaux in which, contrary to all canons of taste I fear (except my own!) I introduced movement though no speech. And I confess that I was struck with the power they displayed 'under the stimulus and influence of a great idea'.

The curtain rose on a bare cottage room. On a pallet bed lay a slight fragile girl of seventeen, supported in the arms of an anxious mother, Mrs Freed herself, whose lined toilworn face lent itself well to the part of mother, as did the marble whiteness of the young girl whom I chose, to the character of daughter. A sister sat sewing by the bedside, and on a chair close by stood a medicine bottle and a cracked cup. A dip candle flared in the neck of an old bottle, and the two little children played with scraps of wood and broken crockery on the floor in front. No need to label the scene as 'The Drunkard's Home'.

In the next scene the girl lay covered with white blossoms, of which the little ones' pinafores were full, while the sister laid the flowers on with reverent hands and the mother knelt weeping by the bedside. Then the scene changed to the inside of the public house where four men, with Freed the father of the dead girl amongst them, sat drinking.

All the parts taken by others than the Freeds themselves were acted by other members of my Bible classes, and in explaining to the men what I wanted I warned them against over-acting. I begged them to remember that there must be nothing ludicrous in either dress or manner in this scene, and I confess to having been amazed at their power of hitting the exact note I wanted.

A little 'feast' in the knot of the red handkerchief, a little devil-me-care in the manner in which they frothed the ale in their glasses – there was nothing overacted, and when from behind the scenes, visible to the others before the father himself discovered it, a white-winged angel crossed the stage, and laying a hand on his shoulder whispered a word in his ear, he rose in dismay. Dashing his glass against the wall he broke it into a thousand fragments, showing real insight as he stumbled to his feet, and with bowed head and a slight lurch in his walk left the room. I had feared a drunken reel, but there was only the slightest hint of his condition in his unsteady step.

The next scene showed him kneeling by the bedside, his face buried in his hands. The children with awed faces stood by, while the wife's arm was round her repentant husband. The final scene, dear to the teetotaller but far less picturesque, found the whole family gathered round a neatly spread and plentiful tea table, while the husband leaned over his wife's shoulder and poured his week's wages into her lap.

Last year I came upon some words in Stead's introduction to his translation of the Ammergau Play of 1910, and looking back on this little play and remembering that all the actors in it were absolutely untrained, that the scene in the public house with the difficulty of getting the men together had not even been rehearsed, I fully endorsed his words, "It is not native capacity that is lacking to mankind, it is the guiding brain, the patient love, the careful education and the stimulus and inspiration of a great idea. But given these, every village of country yokels, from Dorset to Caithness, might develop artists as noble and as devoted as those of Ober Ammergau".

At the time I little guessed how poignant was the stimulus that had resulted in the request that I would write a play on the temperance question. Only when I saw poor Freed sinking into habits of intemperance did it come to my knowledge that as a young man he had been given to drink, and that it was his wife's greatest wish to get him to sign the pledge as a safeguard against a possible return to old habits. And how true her instinct had been! As soon as trouble came, the long disused habit asserted itself again and added yet another drop to the cup of bitterness that was put to their lips.

What strange mixtures we all are. How good and evil, pride and humility, gentleness and hardness, nay even love and hatred, strive for the mastery in people of strong character. But where, as in this case, there is a solid foundation, though for a time evil may triumph and the whole fabric may seem to totter to its fall, it will right itself at last. Slowly, as all good things grow, the true, the good, the beautiful, will reassert themselves, and the brave soul will rise softened and purified from what threatened to be the crumbling ruins of a spoilt life. A long illness, which gave the vicar the chance of saying a few straight but loving words, and the weakness which followed, brought humility with it. The temptation to drink was again trodden underfoot, and who can doubt that good will be triumphant in the end, nay one can *see* the better spirit growing in the gentler expression and softened voices of the whole family. And the little grandchildren who climb lovingly on the grandfather's knee assuredly have sounded the depths of a warm heart and a kindly nature.

Chapter VIII

THE LONELY LUNATIC

Suth GOD hath the myghte
To geven eche a whit wit
Welthe and his hele
And sufferth suche as gou
Hit semeth to mine inwith
Hit arn as hus aposteles such puple
Other as his preye disciples . . .
Suche manere men . . .
We should have hem to house
And help them when thei come
For hit areu mueyr mouthed men
Mynstrales of hevene
And GODES boys, bordiours.

Since God is strong enough
To give to each man wit, wealth, and health
And lets them go, these lunatics, they are I think
His apostles, His private disciples;
Such men we should have home
And help them when they come.
They are merry singers, heaven's minstrels,
God's boys, jesters . . .

The Vision of Piers Plowman

"Insanity is often the logic of an accurate mind overtaxed . . . We frequently see persons in Insane Hospitals sent there in consequence of what are called religious mental disturbances. I confess that I think better of them than of many who hold the same notions, and keep their wits and appear to enjoy life well."

Autocrat of the Breakfast Table

"Pray sit down." The invitation was accompanied by a wave of the hand intended evidently to imply the hospitable desire that I should

Victorian photograph of Black Mill, now demolished.

choose that one among the many easy chairs which best suited my ideas of comfort.

I looked around the meagre cottage room in which not a vestige of furniture was to be seen – neither chair, table, bench nor stool. The only possible resting place, if *resting* place it could be called, consisted of the high narrow ledge (it could not be called window seat) which is so often filled to overflowing with geraniums, fuchsias and musk, but in this case was as bare as the rest of the room and as scrupulously clean.

I hitched myself sideways on this apology for a seat while my hostess locked the door behind me and put the key into her pocket. To enter that door I had had to step over a wilderness of nettles, thistles and long grass which grew in wild confusion between the stones of the broken step, and I was now alone with my hostess, whom I knew to be out of her mind and who had herself told me that she had spent some years of her life in a lunatic asylum for knocking down a clergyman with her umbrella! But I cannot say that I felt afraid, though it did just occur to me that she had at least the key as a weapon of offence while I had no defensive one whatever. But though this was my first visit to her in her own domain, she had often been to me in mine and we were great friends.

She had come some little time before to ask if I wanted anyone to do occasional cooking, or even charring. She did not mind what she did; she was a good cook, she said, and could make soups and entrées and sweets and send up a first class dinner for a large party. The very last thing unfortunately that I in my little home needed.

She was an interesting looking woman with a keen intelligent face, and little tricks of speech unusual in her class. She would give me a piece of information, or make a humorous remark, and add, with a quick gesture and a twinkle in her eye, "You take me?"

She had come a few weeks ago to the empty cottage she was now occupying, with only a little handbag, but had said that her furniture would arrive on the following day. It never did arrive, and the possession of it was probably one among the many hallucinations from which she was suffering. Anyway she continued to speak with a cheerful certainty of its coming – to the end of the chapter.

She washed in the brook, kept her hair (which was as short as a boy's) always well brushed and tidy, and though her dress was poor it was always clean and neat.

She gave me an interesting account of herself and the cause of her quarrel with her clergyman, which apparently arose from the much vexed question of her seat in church being changed. As far as I could make out they were standing together on the steps of the church and she gave him an unexpected push which made him lose his balance. She seemed to think the whole story a good joke and evidently enjoyed the recital of it.

She had been happy in the asylum, she told me. Everyone had been good to her and they had offered her the post of cook to the institution if she would have stayed on. But she refused. She had an idea that she was heir to a fortune of which she had been defrauded and she carried on a long correspondence with her lawyer on the subject, or believed that she did so.

I wrote to the asylum to which she had been confined and got a good account of her from the doctor who said they were sorry that she had refused the offer of the position of cook for which she was well fitted. This confirmed her own account of herself as capable of sending up a first rate dinner. He also spoke of her as thoroughly respectable and as having no suicidal or homicidal tendencies.

The author's photograph of hedgerow trees.

We had many long and interesting conversations, but as this was the first time I had penetrated to her domain, so also was it the first time that I had realised the state of poverty and desolation in which she lived. Yet I felt sure that it would be difficult to offer her help. I talked to her about her expected furniture, and contrived without hurting her sensibilities to offer the loan of a saucepan and blanket and a few little things 'till it came'. A friend and I took her offerings of eggs and other things 'till she had settled her business with her lawyer'.

She was always cheerful, humorous and interesting, and had many tales, amusing, pathetic or tragic, of her sojourn in the asylum. Of her time there she spoke without reserve, and she also told me of her delusion – that most common and painful one – that she had committed the unforgivable sin. It did not seem to distress her now, indeed I never saw her look cast down or troubled even when telling me that she would have had a good income had she not been cheated in some mysterious way by a grasping relation.

I was taken into her bedroom to see a print dress that she was making preparatory to taking a place in service. Bed there was none, nor mattress, nor blanket, nor wrap of any kind. Only on the banister that as is so often the case with old cottages railed off the bedroom from the stairs, hung the skirt of a dress. This she said she put over her when she lay down on the floor to sleep, and though it was late in the autumn and the nights were chilly, she assured me with a cheerful smile that she was 'warm, quite warm, too hot sometimes'. Nevertheless she accepted graciously the loan of the blanket 'till the furniture should come'. On the hearth, in which there was no grate, she had put a few bricks, and on the bricks stood a spirit kettle and my saucepan. This and her handbag were absolutely the only things in the room, save a very neatly made and pretty print dress just finished by herself for her outfit as a servant. She watched me keenly as I admired the dress, a dark blue cotton with a little white sprig upon it, and asked me anxiously whether I liked it. When I told her that I thought it very pretty and well chosen she asked sharply, "You don't see anything odd about it?"

"Certainly not", I said.

"You don't think there's something odd in the pattern?"

Again I said, "No", and told her I liked it very much indeed.

She asked me, "What do you think the white sprig is?"

I answered her, "It seems to me they are daisies".

"And it's all right?" she asked again, "I haven't been cheated? It is really a flower and nothing odd?"

I could but repeat that I saw nothing odd, and that I thought it especially pretty, and this time she seemed satisfied.

There she lived in her empty house for about three months, I suppose, and then getting an answer to an advertisement she prepared to go to a situation in London as cook.

Every day she struck me as less and less sane, and yet withal wonderfully capable. How would it end? Would she be able to keep the situation she had obtained, or would she drift back into the asylum?

It was with many doubts and fears that I walked down with her to the station to see her off. She promised to write to me and, stooping from the carriage as the train was about to start, she kissed me – a greeting for which I was hardly prepared – and was gone and I saw her no more.

The blanket carefully folded was left with a neighbour for me, and after a few days I received a brief letter telling me that when she got to her situation she was met at the door by the mistress of the house and told that the house had been robbed. She continued, "I did but say that I did not see any signs of thieves and they turned me out of the house".

What was really the case, whether the whole story was the creation of her vivid imagination, what happened or how it happened I never

Old photograph of a local heavily-timbered farmhouse.

knew. I wrote again and told her I hoped she would let me hear from her now and then, but I never heard again, and I am inclined to hope as well as think that she probably found her way once more to the asylum, where she was already a favourite and where her powers being employed she was valued and happy.

Certainly it has been my fate to be thrown rather unusually with those of unsound mind, though I am thankful that I have never had to deal with a raving or dangerous lunatic. Even during the time that I was visiting this poor lonely woman in her empty house, and she was constantly coming to me, another poor thing similarly afflicted was coming every few days to pour out her troubles to me, which consisted in her being 'scandalised' by her neighbours, that is to say being spoken falsely about behind her back. Indeed the two met on my doorstep, and only by keeping both in play, one in the dining room and the other in the kitchen, could I attend to both. The 'scandalised' lady informed me that she had come to bring me some plums and proceeded to draw from her pocket a not overclean pocket handkerchief, a brass thimble, a few other odds and ends and half a dozen ripe plums, for which I thanked her profusely but which I need hardly say I did not eat.

She, poor soul, got better without having to be, as the poor pathetically express it, 'put away', and continued to live at home, only being a little unlike her neighbours and never becoming either incapable or dangerous.

The nearest approach to a raving lunatic with whom I had to do, lived in the tiny one storey cottage of the mill close by.

It was a Sunday afternoon and the pattering of little feet and the tinkling of the school bell told that the children were on their way to school, when I heard what I believed to be the scream of a drunken woman. It was during hop-picking, when such sounds were alas not uncommon and the road past my house saw many sad scenes. Indeed but a short time before, I had seen a picturesque yet pathetic sight. A woman, clothed in hopper's rags and with huge 'clouted' shoes, was dancing in front of a cart, skilfully and gracefully, and in spite of being quite tipsy she contrived to cross and recross the road almost under the horse's hooves, performing intricate steps all the time without getting knocked down. Surely at some time of her life she must have danced on the stage, for even the rough nailed boots could not make her steps other than elegant or her postures other than graceful.

A drunken scream then I thought it was that I heard, and I ran to my gate to protect the little ones who were on their way to school.

There at her gate stood my poor neighbour the miller's wife, her face deadly white and terror stamped on every feature. As she saw me she wrung her hands and cried, "Oh, my good woman, my good woman, come and help me, my son has gone out of his mind."

The miller's family belonged to some sect of Particular Baptists who I believe hold that only those who possess their own peculiar tenets can be saved. Whether this belief had, as it well might, driven them mad, or whether insanity would account for the holding of such a doctrine, I cannot say, but certain it is that the mother herself and each child in turn had developed symptoms of insanity at one or other time of their lives. The son in question was a baker, whose hard work and long hours in the hot atmosphere of the bakehouse had completely unnerved him. He had come home to rest and quite suddenly had gone off his head. And with the idea that the two chapels that belonged to his sect were both on fire he had broken the window in a frenzy and rushed out to the rescue.

Whether the fact that the two chapels were some five miles apart and in opposite directions made him uncertain in his movements I cannot say, but with the curious instinct of the working man that he can do nothing bareheaded he had actually paused when half out of the window to look for his cap!

The mother, with a degree of self control hardly to be expected from her previous history, introduced me with, "Here's a lady come to see you. You know Miss Rivers."

Perhaps the shock of a stranger's presence made him pull himself together but certainly it changed his thoughts. I shook hands with him and remarked that though we were such near neighbours I did not think I knew him.

"Oh, but I know you," he replied, "You see, when you came to live here I was out in the world, but I've often seen you."

Somehow, and I do not remember how, I induced him to draw a chair to the fire and light his pipe, knowing that if anything would soothe him that would. Then I started a discussion on smoking in general and women's smoking in particular, on which we both entirely agreed. Meantime his mother slipped out to call her neighbours, and by the time they arrived he was quietly smoking and talking and apparently much like other people. But they had to sit up with him all night as he got fits of raving, and the following morning he was sent to the asylum where I fear he still is.

Whether in Heddingden there was an unusual amount of intermarriage I do not know, but there was certainly an unusual amount of insanity.

Now, however, with a good train service and plenty of communication with the outside world, one hopes that the present generation will not suffer from that common scourge of out-of-the-way country parishes. But in enumerating some among the many cases of lunacy with which I have been acquainted one must remember that by far the largest proportion were imported, and the fact that I came across them may possibly be accounted for by the strange attraction I seem to possess for those of unsound mind.

It is a gift, if gift it is, which I do not regret, though I am thankful to have been spared the most terrible and tragic side of that most terrible and tragic of all diseases, especially as I have very little faith in my own powers of taming a dangerous lunatic.

Chapter IX

THE NEW CURATE

"No person whatever shall be admitted without visible queerity in his aspect, or peculiar cast of countenance."

The Act of Deformity, Rule I of the 'Ugly Club',
Sir Roger de Coverley

'Visible queerity' – yes, that would describe our curate; so let these words stand without contradiction at the head of my chapter.

Our vicar overworked himself and broke down after a long bout of influenza; a curate was engaged for a year to give him a chance of comparative rest. But about the engaging of the curate there was one difficulty: where was he to live?

Being a woman of 'a certain age', with a spare room at my disposal, I told the vicar that if he got a *young* man and a *gentleman* I would if he liked take him in, but stipulated that I must see him before committing myself.

At length a man presented himself who sounded likely – an older man than our vicar, a married man and one who could afford to take half of a semi-detached house in the village. But as the vicar wished him to see the place before engaging him I was asked to give him a bed for the night.

As I rose to greet him I found myself confronted by an elderly man of unpleasant aspect, soapy manner and a fearful squint. Before he had been five minutes in the house he had asked, "Do you let lodgings?" and when I said "No" he rejoined, "I thought I might be very comfortable here." He then proceeded to enquire what was the vicar's private income, how old his wife was, and whether (my mourning dress being no deterrent) my father and mother were alive. He asked as nearly as possible, without actually putting the question in so many words, my income and my age. Finally, and how we got on to the subject I do not remember, we discussed the Athanasian Creed, and when I got up to give him his bed candle and wish him goodnight

The Parish Church of St Peter and St Paul, showing little difference between an old postcard and a photograph taken in 1985. The spire has been removed, as has the creeper growing on the walls, and to the left there is now an avenue of chestnuts which were planted to commemorate Queen Victoria's Diamond Jubilee.

he gave me to understand that he was enjoying himself so much that he did not care to go to bed, and that we thought exactly alike on doctrinal subjects, so *when* he came – no 'if' – we should be great friends.

His person and manner, his character (if I was right in my reading of it) were so odious that I felt certain our good vicar would not think of engaging him. So with no fear of ever having to meet him again I played the agreeable hostess, and as in duty bound made him as happy as I could. If he wished to sit up till two o'clock it would not hurt me to be late for once, so I put the unlighted candle down and prepared to listen.

He breakfasted with me the next morning and I saw him depart with an inward sensation of thankfulness. To my dismay I found that in spite of the fact that his wife had gauged his character exactly as I had the vicar engaged him, and he and his very queer wife settled down in the village.

Naturally, after the encouragement I had given him, he made a dead set at me, and I found out my folly too late to do anything but regret it. When he proceeded to make himself agreeable, as he evidently believed, I was his 'Bishop' and his 'Tower of strength', and when someone spoke of my little house as a 'nutshell' he rolled on me languishing eyes and said, "But with a precious kernel." In vain I retorted that I was not aware that it had ever been occupied by a colonel, but nothing would stop his fulsome compliments, and for some time he continued to call constantly though I was always 'out'.

Later the vicar's wife expressed her opinion of him in the trenchant unflattering and none too refined words, "He is a licentious pig!"

His wife was hardly more agreeable than he, and on one occasion came down to greet me when I called in a dressing jacket and a velvet hat! It was said that the too frequent recourse to the bottle was at the bottom of her oddities, but whatever the cause there were few people save my next door neighbours who were sorry when they departed.

"May I call you sister?" he asked of the faithful friend of the Dudleys when he met her there on one occasion, and he always spoke of the Dudleys themselves as 'Sweet Sisters'. Poor souls, with all their good qualities that was an epithet that could not justly be applied to them, and I am ashamed to confess that on one occasion, when Christobel threw herself on my shoulder and kissed me, grieved as I was for her sorrows I went home and washed! No, 'sweet' was *not* the word.

One of the many ponds. Local residents have suggested that this early photograph may show one of the ponds, now filled in, by the roadside close to Rushford Manor.

On the day of his departure I happened to be at the station to meet a friend, and to my annoyance she got out of the very carriage in which he had seated himself, so that it was impossible to pretend that I did not see him. So without attempting to shake hands I said, "I hope you will be happy in your new home."

He leered at me with those unholy eyes and replied, "If you are sorry to say goodbye I shall come again some day." I pretended not to hear, and was turning away when he forced me to give him 'the cut direct' by beginning again, "*If* you're sorry to say goodbye . . ." I stood my ground, looked him full in the face and made no rejoinder, and the train carried him away. I never saw him again, nor did he ever return to claim the furniture which was held in pawn by his landlady for arrears of rent. Every quarter the rent was demanded, and every quarter he wrote a letter to his 'Dear Christian sister' to say he was sure she was too good and kind to press him. How it ended I am not sure, but I think his furniture still graces his former lodgings.

Perhaps the squint that they shared in common makes me place Miss Vandeleur next on my list of oddities. A woman of nearly eighty she looked at the house next door to me with the intention of taking it. Indeed she quite believed that she was accepted as tenant, and took measurements for carpets and curtains in the full belief that she would be my neighbour.

As an acquaintance of the Dudleys' faithful friends, herself a lady and a woman of good family, I expected to find Miss Vandoleur's breeding equal to her fine name. I asked her to luncheon on the day she came to look at the house, as the trains were awkward and she had a cross-country journey to get home.

I was not favourably impressed and unfortunately she *was*. I fear I must confess that I seem to possess an attraction for queer people, especially for those who have a vein of insanity in them. So many odd or insane persons have taken to me that it has become a standing joke with my nephews and niece that "it is dangerous to be fond of Aunt Penelope, it argues a crook in the brain!"

Miss Vandileur could not be called insane but she was very very queer, and she, like 'the licentious pig' had a fawning manner and a flattering tongue.

Happily – *most* happily for *me* – though I honestly think she was ill used in the matter, the house she had chosen was let over her head, and I was not doomed to her perpetual presence. She ended by taking rooms at the doctor's house further down the road, but she was constantly and never endingly coming to call.

She was very deaf and had a deep sepulchral voice, and started many most remarkable ideas with which I seldom or never agreed. But as she never heard my replies distinctly I believe she gave her friends to understand that Miss Rivers' views entirely coincided with her own, and she called me, so I was told, a 'delightful Being'.

One day as she was sitting at tea with me (poor old lady, one could but pay her that little civility) she said, "Is it not interesting to see prophecy being fulfilled perpetually as we can do so plainly nowadays?"

I replied that it would be very interesting indeed, but that with the exception of the exodus of the Jews from Europe towards the Holy City, which *did* seem likely to fulfil the promises of their return to their own land, I was afraid I had not seen the fulfilment to which she alluded.

"Oh," she rejoined in her deep impressive voice, "I see it going on constantly. We are told that at the Last Day we shall meet the Lord in the air, and with this wonderful invention of flying machines one sees how this will be possible."

Louis Wain's sketch of Stephen Langton's stone bridge, entitled 'An Oast House'.

I confess that the thought of our flipping about on flying machines at the Judgment Day seemed to me so grotesque, not to say irreverent, that I could hardly keep my countenance, and I certainly felt that if a mechanical contrivance were needed to fulfil so poetical a prophecy I would willingly forgo its fulfilment. I ventured to say that to me the idea seemed too irreverent to be contemplated seriously.

She was very much taken aback and could only reiterate again and again, "Oh, no, not irreverent." This was some seven or eight years ago and she has left Heddingden now, but the strides which aviation has made in the last few years must indeed fill her with joy, and strengthen her still more in her belief that she is personally a spectator of the fulfilment of prophecy.

Some time after she had put forth this remarkable suggestion, an earthquake in some neighbouring country – I forget where – was described as having so altered the face of the land that the spire of a church unseen before from that special point of view had now come into sight.

Miss Vanduleur's description of it, culled as she believed from that very account, was scenic and grandiloquent in the extreme.

"It was *heaved* up," she announced in her tragic voice and with the gradual raising of both hands as though engaged in lifting tons of earth, "Heaved up into sight. It was all *ve*-ry remarkable."

Indeed it would have been had it been true. It did not seem worth discussing with a deaf person who was so fully persuaded of the truth of it and who got so much pleasure out of her persuasion. So I said, "Indeed?" and found that I was supposed by the small world of

The same scene in 1985. The river Beult flows more freely beneath Stephen's Bridge, though the tree on the far side is now massive and there is no sign of the Oast House.

Heddingden to have understood the newspaper account after her rendering.

She positively haunted those to whom she took a fancy, and used to pay such frequent visits to a neighbour of mine that she became an intolerable nuisance. They had no servant, but in vain did the mistress of the house fly to the back regions and refuse to hear the bell. Miss Vandaleur followed her to the back door and finally took to bringing her cap with her, and with no invitation settled herself in their drawing room for the afternoon. Hints were unavailing, and at last the master of the house wrote and told her plainly that she was not wanted. It was an unfortunate thing to be driven to do, but I can hardly blame him for doing it.

As one after another tired of her she fixed herself like a limpet on some newcomer, till the last acquaintance being in his turn sucked dry she attached herself with her wonted adhesiveness to yet another – and another. Happily for me, like the historical 'rat that was seen brewing in the air' I had 'nipped it in the bud', and though wearied by her importunity had never to resort to positive rudeness to get rid of her.

It would seem that should Louis Wain be able to see his sketch alongside a 1985 photograph, the only differences he would notice would be the change in name from Ye George Inn to the George and Dragon, the different position of the inn sign, and the price of a pint of ale.

Chapter X

THE HAUNTED HOUSE

"Whilst I am following one character, it is ten to one but I am crossed in my way by another, and put up such a variety of odd creatures in both sexes, that they foil the scent of one another and puzzle the Chase."

Sir Roger de Coverley

My next 'oddity' was a link with the past.

In our old home in the Midlands stands a pretty house that goes by the name of 'The Manor', though I believe there is no foundation for the name. It is rather a picturesque house, embowered in trees and with a gate in the churchyard wall which gives the impression that it ought to be the vicarage. When first I remember it it was desolate enough, overgrown with wild creepers and unpruned trees, out of repair and with blisters of damp and fallen plaster on the walls. For its owner was insane, and the house in Chancery, and who does not know what that word implies?

Then one day we found men at work on it. The house was let, and strange to say the father of the man who had taken it was also insane and he himself was a ward in Chancery, dependent on an annual allowance, which though quite enough to live on liberally in a small way was but a small proportion of the inheritance which would be his at his father's death. They were pleasant people, friendly and kind, and their three children were interesting and grew greatly attached to us.

It was not long before we made acquaintance with his mother, and the outcome of her visit was an invitation to my sister and myself to spend a fortnight with her at Morton Hall, their old family place in Blankshire.

The house was built upon a rock overlooking a little brawling stream. It was moated and had once possessed a drawbridge and portcullis, though the latter had disappeared altogether and the former, now dry, was crossed by a stone bridge.

The massive oak door admitted one to a large low hall, panelled like most of the rest of the house with black oak, which with its raftered ceiling and heavy beams was so dark that when its mistress read family prayers there at nine o'clock in the morning candles had to be placed on the table at her side. A wide oak staircase, with very handsome carved banisters and shallow winding stairs, ascended to the right, and in odd out of the way corners stood men in armour which in the dusk of the evening had rather a ghostly effect. Swords, helmets, pikes, spurs and other trophies of former days graced the walls. The open fireplace, flanked by solid settles, held huge fire dogs, on which doubtless in winter the great logs would crackle merrily; but it was summer when we were there.

The low mullioned windows looked out over the edge of a precipice to the stream below, and the raftered ceiling, quaint with rich carvings here and there did much to intercept the little light the narrow lattice could give. On the left another door opened into the library, a small square room lined with books from floor to ceiling, fitted and furnished with black oak and darker even than the hall. At the end of the hall furthest from the entrance one opened a door into a modern drawing room with wide windows looking over the cliff. It was painted white, and bright with sunshine and every cheerful contrivance for comfort and convenience with bright flower beds below. Charming as the old oak was it was perhaps natural that Mrs Auguetil lived chiefly in the more modern drawing room. Yet she was eminently fitted in person and character to the more rich and sombre surroundings of the older part of the house.

Ample in her proportions she was also wide in her sympathies, and broad in her interpretation of the duties entailed upon her by her position.

'Dame Eleanor Auguetil' would have sounded much more in keeping with her appearance and outlook on life than the more modern appellation, and she ruled her strange household with wide sympathies and a firm hand.

And a strange household indeed it was.

It seemed as if the life of the inmates by some curious law of nature were an exponent of the features of the house itself. For it was not the state rooms alone that had an air of mystery about them and which suggested strange and weird histories. The wide staircase led to quaint old bedrooms, of which one was of course haunted, and the long passage ended in an oubliette used, so tradition said, more than once to get rid of a troublesome acquaintance.

In one of the rooms Cromwell had slept before the battle of Chester, while his Ironsides were quartered in the beautiful old buildings still used as stables, coach houses or barns. For the house belonged to one of the generals of Cromwell's army, whose signature may be found attached to the death warrant of King Charles the First, and whose seal, used on that same warrant, is still preserved in the family.

Cromwell's room remains intact. The heavy four-poster bed has a legend on the tester still to be read by the occupant, which runs after this fashion:

"He that lacks mercy, mercy shall miss
But he shall have mercy, that merciful is."

And in the three-light window is engraved another legend:

"My Brother Henry shall heir the land
My Brother Frank be at his command
My Brother Jack shall do that
Which all the world shall wonder at."

And truly may the world have wondered, for it was the hand of John Bolton Auguetil that signed the fatal document that sent his King to the block.

One wonders what effect that legend may have on the future of my three little friends, Henry, Frank and Jack, of the present day.

The walls of the room are hung with tapestry in which the daughter of Pharaoh and her maidens, with lead coloured complexions, among impossible trees and bullrushes and by an impossible stream, find the child Moses in an impossible ark. On the bed yet lies the self same quilt of silk patchwork which once covered the great Cromwell. And in that room, and in that bed, I too have slept, and wonderful to say was haunted by no strange visions and troubled by no ill dreams.

Next door is the haunted room itself and for a few nights my sister and I shared its ghostly solitude. Yet even there our slumbers were undisturbed. And yet enough had happened in that house to give cause for many a haunting fear, for not the oubliette alone was accountable for the destruction of an enemy: the moat had its secrets too.

It was the old story of the puritan maiden and her Royalist lover, of a dark night and a dark deed, of a raised drawbridge and the disappearance of man and horse. And whatever additions the story may have accumulated, as it passed from mouth to mouth, this at least is sure – in comparatively modern times, when the moat was drained, there was found the skeleton of man and horse to give credence to the story.

And even when we stayed within its beautiful old walls, tragedy was still at work, and strange deeds were being enacted and strange lives lived which harmonised well with its outward aspect. For shut off in a distant wing, with a male attendant, lived the master of all this beauty and romance, a hopeless lunatic.

The story of his old world courtship was one that would account for much of the tragedy that followed. It told of a young girl flattered by the attentions of a dark and fascinating stranger, the son of a county magnate, in whose company the etiquette of the day forbade her ever being alone, a servant walking behind them even when the lovers were wandering together in the garden. A marriage followed a short engagement, and then during the wedding tour the bride made the discovery that the bridegroom was insane.

Two sons were born of this union, before the father was found dancing before the open window on the point of throwing his eldest child over the precipice. He had already more than once threatened his wife's life with a carving knife, but her strong personality had hitherto kept him in check. This last attempt however brought matters to a climax and he was sent to the asylum. Every month his wife visited him there, but she was never allowed to be in the room alone with him as he was both violent and sullen, and once even in the presence of his keeper had sprung upon her. He never spoke, and probably at the time I knew him had lost the power of speech. He had been a musician, but now spent his days in confinement in striking two notes on the piano with which he was provided till the ivories were worn away. But he never actually played again, nor ever touched any but those two keys. For over thirty years he had spent his existence in this fashion, but within a year or two of the time of our visit to Morton Hall, he being supposed to be no longer dangerous, his courageous wife took him out of the asylum and put the wing of the house which I have described at the disposal of himself and his keeper. Every day, wet or dry, they took their constitutional; every evening after dinner he came into the library, played 'Beggar me Neighbour' and stayed for family prayers. If spoken to he made a noise more animal than human. If he won the game, as if possible it was contrived that he should do, his eyes glittered with joy. If his attention was called to any object his eyes followed the direction indicated, but he never moved his head.

When he rose from his knees after prayers, and everyone wished him goodnight, he responded with the curious sound, more grunt than speech, which was his only mode of speech, and left the room with his attendant.

Every day 'Dame Eleanor' poured out tea for him in his own room and talked to him of any little event that had happened in the course of the day. But she elicited no response beyond the usual grunt and seemed to awake no interest in his dormant mind. Yet with this weight upon her life she contrived to keep up her health and spirits, her sturdy good sense and wonderful care for the hopes and fears, joys and sorrows, of her neighbours.

No one else already weighted with such a burden would have added to it the care of a deaf and dumb servant who, when in a temper, which was not seldom, would utter piercing screams, and who always accompanied manual labour with sounds and expressive noises to match the hardness of her task. As a groom hisses as he rubs down a horse, so did Phoebe grunt as she swept floors or dusted banisters.

Dame Eleanor's second son had crowned a wild youth by a hasty marriage with a woman inferior to himself in position, and when we were there the little son of this ill-assorted couple was spending, as he always did, his holidays with his grandmother. The child was a spoilt disobedient boy of nine or ten and not in any way interesting, but I used to take him off his grandmother's hands by playing hide and seek with him all over the house in the gloaming before it was time for lights to be brought in. It was rather unnerving when the dark little figure pounced out with a yell from some hidden and unexpected nook or from behind some grim warrior in armour or rushed down the shallow oak stairs from the gallery above.

His grandmother paid for his schooling and did all she could to bring him up as a Christian and a gentleman, but home influence was against making him either and it seemed doubtful indeed how the child would turn out.

But when we arrived at Morton Hall three other inmates had been added to the already curious assemblage. Dame Eleanor had brought a baby of a few hours old, wrapped in a blanket, from the side of its dead mother, and the child was a bonnie boy of about nine months old when we were introduced to it, splashing about in its tub with Phoebe in adoring attendance. The father, a very poor clergyman, had tried as best he could to bring up in a 'feeless' fashion the two elder children, but with no one to keep house for him he had at last boarded out the elder, a girl, with a cottage mother, in his parish.

This Louis Wain sketch shows fifteenth century Clothworkers Hall, now known as Shakespeare House and originally the Queen Adelaide Inn.

He and his wife had met abroad. Both were lonely, and the girl was kept persistently in the background by a jealous and worldly mother. Having no home and no education that would fit her to stand alone, she had fallen in love with the penniless curate and he with her. It ended in a runaway match on £10 which she had as pocket money, and the hope that all would be forgiven and forgotten by the incensed parents when the marriage had actually taken place. Needless to say the jealous mother was glad to get rid of a daughter whom she had never loved, and they were left to reap the fruit of their folly.

When we were there the distracted widower was also a guest in the house, and it did not add to the ease of entertaining him to know that he carried a bottle of poison in his pocket and set covetous eyes on the windows that looked over the rocky terrace on to the stream.

Trees and shrubs, and a well maintained village war memorial, have made an identical 1985 picture almost impossible. The high pitched gable remains, as do chimneys and much of the timbering, but the position of many windows has been altered.

Some of us had to keep informal guard over him and to try to make life interesting and if possible even amusing for him.

It was while we were there too that our kind hostess drove over and fetched the little girl from her cottage home to share the generous hospitality of Morton Hall. The child arrived in such a state of dirt and dishevelment that she had to be put into a bath and washed before anything could be done for her amendment. Poor little Ermingard – it went to one's heart to take off the dainty coronetted underclothing and to comb out the tangled hair, and hear the provincialisms which fell from the lips of what should have been a lady-child. And a lady Dame Eleanor determined that she should be, though a lady capable of earning her own livelihood. She had found a school for poor gentlefolks, and it was to get her outfit and send her there at her own expense that this large-hearted woman had brought her to her own home.

We all set to work, and with sewing machine and willing hands we soon got her clothes in order, and shortly after we left the child was placed under the care of the ladies who kept this school. The boy was sent to a school of a like kind by the same kind friend. The baby she adopted, and pinching herself for his sake lest she should rob her grandchildren of their due, she put by a yearly sum for his education and start in life.

Meanwhile while my sister and I were busy with needle and thread Dame Eleanor, who was not a good needlewoman, did her part towards the preparations by adding to an already large correspondence the many letters necessary for the arranging of the children's future.

It was one day when she was so engaged that I asked if I could not take some of the burden of writing off her hands, as she had years before put out her wrist and still found the manual part of it painful.

No, I could not help her as a scribe, but would I pour out tea for Mr Auguetil, try and amuse him and above all encourage him to eat.

Till I had said "Yes" it never even crossed my mind to feel nervous about the task she had set me, but when I entered the room from which anything which could have served as a weapon had been removed, and when I saw the open piano with the two notes with ivory fingerplates worn to the wood, then a little thrill of mingled curiosity and fear came upon me, for he was the first lunatic with whom I had ever held personal communication.

We sat opposite to each other and I poured out his tea and handed him bread and butter, but I was at once faced with an unexpected difficulty. When the plate was handed to him he gave his non-commital grunt and did not attempt to help himself to the contents. I pressed him to take some, helped myself and commented on the excellence of the bread and butter. In vain his eyes looked furtively at me but his hand made no motion towards the plate. I was delivered from my dilemma by the arrival of a magnificent supply of hot buttered toast.

A gleam of interest lighted up his face and this time there was no difficulty in getting him to eat. He took a slice, measured it carefully with his eye, bit exactly into the middle of the slice and laid the rest down. We waited. Taking his spoon he industriously followed imaginary runnels of tea down the sides of his cup and drank his tea, but the discarded toast still remained untouched. At last after waiting his pleasure patiently while his eye fixed itself on the muffin plate in the middle of the table, I tried handing it to him again. In this manner he got through a very respectable quantity, the rejected half of every piece still being left upon the plate.

The tea things were removed and now came the task of entertaining him. I was half a Yorkshire woman, so that I could sing goes without saying, but I never could play, and with all my love of music I could only accompany myself in three simple songs. Would he like me to sing to him? A grunt which might have meant anything, but which I could only hope meant 'yes' was his reply, and with singular rashness – a rashness which I realized too late to alter my intention – I turned my back upon him to sing. What if he, who had been a good performer in his time, angered by my feeble efforts, should spring upon me from behind? The thought was unpleasant! Whether it pleased him or no I cannot say for he made no sign by word or gesture, and his face I could not see. But he did me no bodily injury and I went through my limited repertoire, after which his attendant came. I fled with a certain feeling that by my stupid offer to sing I had taken my life in my hands and might have had to pay for my folly.

Poor man, he passed quietly away some months afterwards, and the noble woman once mistress of the Hall sleeps now under the shadow of the little church in which she was a constant and devout worshipper. The eldest son has come to his inheritance, and the Henry, Frank and Jack of this generation have succeeded to the room with its historic legend.

And what of the child of the ne'er-do-well son? It was he of whom I spoke as a link with the past and who strangely enough was to become one of the 'oddities of Heddingden'.

A very small poorly built house, neither cottage nor villa but partaking of the faults of both, fell vacant, and report said that a 'big doctor' from one of our fashionable seaside resorts was coming to live in it but did not mean to practise. It sounded very unlikely as the house, though new, was singularly shabby in its proportions and had evidently been built with the idea of becoming a small lodging house. This news was followed by a rumour that the new doctor was doubtful as to whether he would patronize church or chapel as it would depend upon who called on him! And then his name leaked out. It was Auguetil.

Though the name is not a common one there were brewers of that name in our county town, and my sister and I settled that he was probably related to them. Still more assured were we that this must be the case when we saw a huge coarse-looking man accompanied by a vulgar little wife come up the hill and take possession of the aforesaid shabby domain. This could be no relation of our Auguetils with their position in their own county and the traditions of their beautiful house, and no relation to the noble old lady who was mistress of Morton Hall.

They settled down, with no servant, and yet daily at the little gate appeared a small dogcart with a high-stepping horse and a tiger behind, in the shape of a boy fresh caught from the plough, dressed in ill-fitting livery with a crest on his buttons. Thus did this strange pair take their daily drives.

Should we call on these unprepossessing people on the remote chance of their belonging to the family with whom we had been so friendly? Or should we take it for granted that they were, and could be, nothing to us? Then one day on passing the house I saw on the tiny gate a huge brass plate on which was engraved 'Alfred Charles Bolton-Auguetil, M.D., F.R.C.P.' etc., and recognised the name of the little boy with whom I had played hide and seek in days gone by behind the mailed figures in the dim light of Morton Hall.

Of course that settled the question and I called. Mrs Auguetil opened the door to me herself and I was confirmed in my previous estimation of her. A lady's maid she might have been, a country innkeeper's daughter or possibly a barmaid, but certainly nothing higher. Yet the first thing that met my eye was a photograph of Morton Hall and I naturally claimed acquaintance. Her husband was called, and came in with a boisterous and free and easy welcome that did not impress me favourably. He was a huge man with a low forehead, the back of the head being abnormally large, and he had no manners and an overweening opinion of his own importance as a Bolton-Auguetil and not a small one of himself personally as a man of parts. The first person singular was the first person in this singular person's estimation, and after singing his own praises he chanted those of the vulgar partner of all these excellences.

Had I noticed the oil paintings that adorned the room? Indeed I had – they arose and smote one in the eye as one entered the door. They were full length portraits begun on a canvas not large enough to contain them, so the lower limbs were curtailed to accommodate themselves to the space allotted to them. The hard highly coloured faces stared out of the heavily gilded frames and they took up the whole size of the walls of the tiny room in which they were hung. Did we know that his wife was an authoress? Well, she was, and a musician too. It was a pity that they had only the dogcart with them, but the brougham with the Auguetil arms on it – mark you – they had parted with, or they would have been happy to have taken me for a drive. Was I a churchman? Ah well, so was his poor grandmother, and very particular she had been to teach him his Catechism. But for all that he had not been fairly treated, the elder branch of the family had got nearly everything, his poor old grandmother could not have meant it, etc., but he would 'give us a call' at church some day, he was not bigoted either way. Oh yes! He would come sometimes – and thus having patted both me and the Church on the back he evidently thought he had done his duty by both.

For old times sake I asked him and his wife to tea but I did not invite anyone to meet them. He enlarged on the happiness it gave him to renew the acquaintance of one with whom he had played as a child, his 'sweetheart' he might say! And he made the statement that he had no intention of practising; far be it from him to take the bread out of the mouths of our other two doctors, but he would doctor the poor people in a friendly way for nothing.

Why then his conspicuous brass plate with his high-sounding name and additions?

My window, open all day long, looked over a triangular bit of lawn on to the high road, and much of the conversation of the passers-by reached me as I sat at work in the room or attended to my beloved garden. Dr Auguetil's voice was not of the gentlest and I could hear him as he hailed everyone he met, gentle or simple, in stentorian tones. "You seem to have a bad cough. Been to the doctor, have you? And you are not better? Now *I* could cure you. I'll give you a box of lozenges and you'll soon be all right."

Soon he had a following of his own and was constantly called in as their regular doctor, sending in his account like other practitioners. He was always to the fore, always on the spot, and certainly lost no opportunity of pushing himself.

Then a strange thing happened. Our old established doctor was driving along a side road to see a distant patient. The road ended in a gate into some fields where a cart track led to the farm he was about to visit. The horse, startled by a rustling in the hedge, and laying itself to the ground like a race horse, took the bit between its teeth and galloped frantically up the road towards the gate. Usually it stood open, but by great mischance that day it was closed and the animal swerved suddenly, plunged into a pond by the roadside, threw his master over his head among the stubs of newly cut willows on the bank – the man also falling to the ground – and broke its own neck and got smothered in the mud.

The man broke three ribs, but it fared yet worse with the master whose face was frightfully cut with the sharp points of the willow stumps. A boy was despatched from the farm to fetch a doctor, and behold when he appeared it was our officious friend! There he was, in an extraordinarily short time, with his bag of surgical instruments in his hand, and with skilful and careful hands he sewed the doctor's wound, brought him home, put him to bed with his own hands, and proposed that he should take his work for him then and there. Happily the lady who kept house for the doctor had the presence of mind to refuse the offer and send to the doctor of another parish who was always summoned in case of need, or small chance would there have ever been of the practice being saved. But, to his credit be it said, the interloper proved really clever, and his skill and promptitude certainly did much to save his patient who for some weeks hovered between life and death.

Nor was this the only occasion on which Dr Auguetil proved himself capable of seizing every opportunity that fate might send him.

The sound of a runaway horse, with the rattle and bump of an empty carriage at its heels, brought me to the window one day, to see a light carriage, the reins trailing on the ground and the pony tearing down the hill. Like a flash it was gone, but tearing after it, bag in hand, hatless and eager, panted Dr Auguetil.

It proved to be only a case of a frightened pony starting off before the driver had taken his place, but there was not a doubt that whatever happened the new doctor would be first in the running.

Yet the wonder to me was that anyone would consent to put himself, or yet more any of his womenfolk, into his hands, clever though they undoubtedly were.

Of his wife's authorship something must be said, for when one opened the pages of her book one found oneself in the midst of high life indeed. Dukes and duchesses, earls and countesses, were as plentiful as blackberries, and indeed a title was the only entrée into the select and aristocratic society with which they abounded. I doubt whether she ever sank so low as a knight or a baron. The names of the actors on this right royal stage savoured of the days of old Romance, and the actors themselves stepped on to the boards covered with diamonds of the first water and wore their strawberry leaves encrusted with precious gems.

But it was the *language* which carried this work of genius into latitudes undreamed of in this work-a-day world.

To say that it was not English was to say little and few even of the readable novels of the present day can lay claim to that title; but it was no language that any being in heaven or earth ever spoke, or will speak, to the end of time. Long words often of her own coining, perhaps still oftener picked up from the inflated language of the servants' hall when it was aping the drawing room. But picked up with terminations or pronunciation never heard in any society one has ever entered, and these words shed their lustre over every page.

How could any publisher have ever consented to take it, or any bookseller to lay it on his counter? One turned to the title page and found it had been privately printed, at the expense one presumed of the fond husband. Such was the work of the talented lady who combined music, painting and literature in her own person.

A few quotations taken at random from her books may be interesting and show to what extent she could lay claim to the title of authoress.

Introducing her characters she gives this description of one of them:

"The Countess was an inexceptionally pleasant hostess."

Of another: "After his College curriculum, he became very obdurate and ran the gauntlet which gave the Earl rather a pessimistic opinion of him."

A dog comes upon the scene and of the heroine it is said, "Shaking its paw vehemently at the same time she scrutinously asked, 'Who is the donor?'"

Of the hero: "As he returned his heart began to elate, with all its effulgence of yore, till he was quite forgetful of self and its lowliness. 'I will duel him out of it yet, the sly old fox,' quoth he."

The careful father expresses his opinion of his daughter's engagement in the following terms: "My darling Child I could not entertain thoughts of you inciting an attachment between Lord Leslie, or imbue your sentiments with his as you are aware he is an apostate. If rumour is true he has also been a sinister in his early days and was a great worry to his dear mother."

To continue: "Dinner was then announced, Nita entering into a very fervid conversation of an exciting logic with young Lieutenant Melmenth as he armed her in to dinner."

Further on Nita and her lieutenant drive to hounds.

"He enquired, 'Do you intend riding to the hounds tomorrow?'

"'If nothing prevents, I have arranged to be at the Meet in time for the throw off of the fox break covert' she ensued.

"'You possess rare talents of a conversant sportswoman.'

"'You are pert,' was her reply, 'You see, I advocate all that is essential to health.'

"'Very illustrous ideas indeed. Can you not be more influential with Celia? . . .'"

Verily these two were as strange a pair as ever entered the Ark in couples.

Note:

In the daily paper of 23 November 1910 appeared the following entry:

"Remarkable evidence was given before the . . . magistrates yesterday, when Dr Auguetil and his wife Louisa were charged with being wandering lunatics. The doctor appeared in the dock without the usual clothing on the upper part of the body, and wore a rug, while his wife was attired in a cap and long overcoat.

"Police Sergeant . . . said he went to the residence of the two defendants on Tuesday night and found that the doctor was inside the house with a gun. The doctor threatened to shoot anyone who approached the house, and going upstairs rested the gun on the ledge of the window. He kept this position for six hours during the night, and kept crying out in a loud voice, 'Murder, murder'. At 2.15 a.m. the doctor came out scantily clad. He had burnt his clothing in front of the house before the Police arrived.

"Police Constable . . . told the court that he had been visiting Dr Auguetil's house since last Thursday. At 5 a.m. that day Mrs Auguetil sent word that her husband intended to kill himself and the two dogs.

"On Monday, the witness continued, he was sent for in a hurry, and found the doctor very excited. He told the witness that he and his wife had had a dream about his dead mother and had seen her with her mouth open and her tongue out, and that he had to strangle his wife. The witness said the doctor apparently attempted to do so, for Mrs Auguetil was in bed, bleeding from the mouth and nose. Mrs Auguetil said it was quite right, she had to be strangled, as she had seen her mother with blood on her. The bedroom was bespattered with blood and there had evidently been a violent struggle.

"On Tuesday night the whole of the countryside was alarmed because of the doctor's cries. 'He could be heard for a mile,' the witness said.

"Evidence was then given in regard to Mrs Auguetil. It was stated that she was brought to the Police Station on Tuesday night by friends, saying that she wished to be burnt at the stake. She had a Bible with her and she said she was an authoress. She walked about with head erect, calling for bread and wine, and did not sleep all night while in the cells. She also made her Will in favour of Police Sergeant . . . and had it witnessed."

Chapter XI

MORAL HEDGEHOGS

"One had as well meddle with a porkpen which hath thorns all over him."

Poet at the Breakfast Table

"A Hedgehog rolled up the wrong way
Tormenting himself with his prickles."

Miss Kilmansegg and her golden Leg

Kent is I believe inhabited chiefly by unadulterated Jutes, and the manners of the unadulterated Jute leave much to be desired!

I had amusing instances of this fact when, together with several other ladies, I was told off to collect money for our testimonial to our then vicar, Mr Stuart. He was perhaps the most popular man in Heddingden, not only amongst church people but with the whole parish. So knowing that many people who went to other places of worship would wish to join in this testimony to their kindly feeling, every house was visited and I took my share in the visitation.

Two of the people who fell to my lot had a private feud with me, one being the very man who had years before tried to put an end to the men's Bible class. The other had discovered me taking a short cut across his fields to my house and had very rudely shouted to me from a distance to "come off".

When I found that these two were apportioned to me I was glad, as I hoped on a nearer acquaintance to be able to make friends with them.

With neither was I successful, but I think that with both of them it was probably quite as much the inclination to button up the waistcoat pocket as the dislike to myself personally that kept them from giving.

Neither were churchmen, though the one of Bible class notoriety had taken to coming to church, partly I think for the pleasure of sitting obstinately in his place when the rest of the congregation rose at the entrance of clergy and choir. Indeed when at a harvest festival the procession, with banners flying, filed into their seats singing a processional hymn, he audibly remarked, "Sit still, sit still, the fools will be in their places soon."

The other man, Mr Unwin, was not even a churchman in name, though like the rest of the village he seemed to appreciate the vicar's pleasant friendly manner. So with some hope of a civil reception when my errand was known, I knocked at the door.

It was opened to me by Mr Unwin himself. "Mr Unwin?" I asked.

"Yes, I'm Mr Unwin." No greeting did he vouchsafe to me, though his daughter had attended my classes for two years.

"May I come in?" I asked.

"I'd rather you stayed where you are," which is to say on the doorstep.

I laughed as I answered, "Oh, well, I can say what I want to say quite well here," and forthwith proceeded to state the cause of my visit.

"No," he said, "I shan't give to Mr Stuart as long as he has candles on the altar."

"Well," I said, "I can quite understand that there may be differences of opinion about them, but as you do not come to church they cannot do *you* any harm, and I think you will agree that Mr Stuart works very hard and does a great deal of good."

"Oh, you think so, do you?"

"I am sure of it, he works so hard that he is constantly breaking down. However," I added, "I have no wish to urge you to give if you would rather not. I only came because we thought no one would care to be left out in case they wished to share in the testimonial. But before I leave I should like to say that I am sorry I trespassed on your fields. The fact is Mr Lawford, the last owner, gave me leave to take the short cut and I continued to do so, which perhaps I ought not to have done."

"Am I Mr Lawford?"

"No," I laughed, "and I suppose I ought to have asked your leave before taking that route, so I do so now."

"Then you won't get it."

"Well," I said, "I am sorry, but that matters very little. I can easily go round, but I hope you will allow me to go to the little wood where I had leave to gather primroses. I won't do any harm."

"Will you do any *good*?"

"Yes," I said, "I think I shall, for I gather them to send to a hospital."

"You, and such as you, always think you're doing good."

"Anyway," I said, "I will do no harm. I will not break hedges or gather mushrooms. In my old home in Northamptonshire we gathered mushrooms and nobody minded."

"Then you'd better go back there," he interjected.

"But as you spawn your fields," I continued, "You may be sure I will not touch yours. Nor will I do any damage."

"You and your crew are always in my fields," he said.

"Indeed," I said, "I have not been in your fields since you turned me off the other day, and as I live alone I don't quite know whom you mean by my 'crew'."

"If it wasn't you it was Miss Edwards." Miss Edwards was a great friend of mine.

"At any rate I am not accountable for other people trespassing," I said, "So I hope you will let me gather primroses as I used to do in Mr Lawford's time."

No, he wouldn't, and then leaked out the cause of the offence. "You don't even know us when you meet us."

"Do you know," I said, "It is quite true. I have never seen Mrs Unwin to my knowledge, and the day you turned me off your land you were so far off that I did not recognise you when you opened the door to me just now. However I shall know you now and I will promise not to cut you again. Goodbye."

A surly grunt was the answer, and rather to my astonishment his daughter continued to come to my classes.

If there was not a sad side to all such misunderstandings this interview would have been wholly amusing. It was too egregiously rude to be anything but funny, but one can never help feeling, "Oh, the pity of it," and I would fain have made friends and felt that all men were in charity with me, as well as my being in charity with all men.

Whenever we met I bade him goodday and he replied with a sidelong nod, but we got no further, for not long after my sister and I left the place and I have never seen him since.

'Father Christmas', as the other old man to whom I was sent was generally called, admitted me without hesitation, and we began upon rose culture in which he was very successful. I had not been so with mine and asked him as to the pruning of them. He pruned early in February but did not recommend my doing so till the middle of

March. "You're quite a great coat colder on the hill than I am here," he remarked. We got on capitally till I disclosed my errand, when he informed me that he did not like the clergy. "Well," I said, "We've had two very good ones here since I came."

"Oh, you called Mr Lawrence good, did you?"

I answered that I certainly did, when he started a disquisition on baptism and declared that Mr Lawrence believed that if one were baptised it did not matter what one's life was like as one would be sure to go to heaven.

As I knew that this was far from Mr Lawrence's views, or any other man's for the matter of that, I said so, but the old man stuck to his opinion and there was no convincing him. "Anyway," I said, "It is to Mr Stuart that we are hoping to give a farewell present, not to Mr Lawrence."

No, he wasn't going to give to Mr Stuart, Mr Stuart did not give anything to him, and then, as in the case of Mr Unwin, the true reason came out. "Why doesn't he get his coal of me. I sell just as good coal as Mr Dobson."

Of course it was useless to fight against such paltry and selfish reasons, so I took my leave having been unsuccessful in both quarters. I then found that I had been told off to tackle both these men as no one else could be found willing to expose himself to the reception he was likely to get.

The poor old man came to a strange end. He grew old and tottery but still used to potter about in his garden with two sticks, and one day he was found face downwards in the little stream that ran at the bottom of his strawberry beds. Everybody was sorry for him and his poor old housekeeper took it much to heart, fearing that she ought not to have let him go out alone.

When his affairs were looked into it was found that he had once lived in luxury, one may almost say upon capital, but that when he died he had come literally to his last five shillings. So died Father Christmas.

It is pleasant to think that these were almost the only people in the parish who did not give, and give gladly. Others might differ in opinion with the *vicar* but all loved the *man*. Churchman or non-conformist, it did not matter, they were glad to testify to the good work he had done and the tactful way in which it had been carried out, and no man could have been lamented more than he was when

Ellen M. Poole's pencil drawing of The Manor, Welford, dated 1874, see p.103.

he was called to a larger sphere of labour, though to an even poorer living, in one of our great Midland towns.

And this has been the case with several of our vicars. They have worked for a few years with us and then been moved on to harder work and less pay.

But that could only be done where they had something, however little, of their own on which to depend. For ours is one of those livings, poor at the best, whose value depending much upon hops decreases every year. Foreign hops have killed both the farmer and the parson and the land is going steadily down, so that what was once a livelihood is now barely a living, and one is reminded of the ancient name which part of the village still bears and is inclined to call it 'Starveden'.

It was with mingled feelings of joy and sorrow that I heard not long ago that our last vicar Mr Courtney had just been presented to a rectory only a few miles away, but with a better stipend.

He was a delicate highly-strung man, earnest and devout but sadly hampered by bad health, a large family and small means.

How happy it is that people generally marry their opposites. What he would have done without his clever cheery wife, with whom he ran away when they were hardly more than boy and girl, I cannot think, but towards the end even she showed signs of strain. Constant care and anxiety had begun to trace lines on the singularly fair and youthful face as she watched her husband's struggle with failing health and a difficult parish. His doctor's expression, "They are expecting a greyhound to do bulldog's work" described the position exactly.

As to Mrs Courtney you could hardly believe that she had reached middle life, and had had a hard battle of it too, when you saw her in her Sunday school of a hundred infants, half a dozen clinging to her skirts and looking up into her face for a smile. Or watched her showing the maypole children how to dance, with a far lighter step than their own, or heard her taking the comic parts in the Shakespeare readings they themselves had instituted, with the zest and spirit of a girl.

Few visits have been happier than those I have paid to them in their frugal but hospitable home, where wit and kindness reigned supreme, where all who came were welcome, and old friends of all classes flocked to see me as freely as if I had been in my own house.

With the departure of the last of the vicars of Heddingden whom I have known personally, it seems fitting to close my reminiscences.

It is pleasant to look back to the many kind friends who are left, to the ever open door of the vicarage, and in saying a regretful farewell to our home of twenty years to think of the welcome that always awaits one in the parish.

12 March 1912

US BARGEMEN by **A.S. Bennett.** A new book of sailing barge life around Kent and Essex from the author of 'June of Rochester' and 'Tide Time'. ISBN 207. £6.95.

THE GILLS by **Tony Conway.** A history of Gillingham Football Club. 96 large format pages packed with old photographs. ISBN 266. £5.95. **BARGAIN OFFER £1.95.**

A VIEW OF CHRIST'S COLLEGE, BLACKHEATH by **A.E.O. Crombie, B.A.** ISBN 223. £6.95.

JUST OFF THE SWALE by **Don Sattin.** The story of the barge-building village of Conyer. ISBN 045. £5.95.

TEYNHAM MANOR AND HUNDRED (798-1935) by **Elizabeth Selby, MBE.** ISBN 630. £5.95.

THE PLACE NAMES OF KENT by **Judith Glover.** A comprehensive reference work. ISBN 614. £7.50 (also available in paperback. ISBN 622. £3.95)

LARGE FORMAT PICTORIAL PAPERBACKS

GOUDHURST: A Pictorial History by **John T. Wilson, M.A.** ISBN 3026. £2.95.

A PICTORIAL STUDY OF ALKHAM PARISH by **Susan Lees and Roy Humphreys.** ISBN 3034. £2.95.

THE MOTOR BUS SERVICES OF KENT AND EAST SUSSEX – A brief history by **Eric Baldock.** An illustrated history from 1899 to 1984 containing 146 photographs. ISBN 959. £4.95.

ROCHESTER FROM OLD PHOTOGRAPHS – see under hardbacks.

PEMBURY IN THE PAST by **Mary Standen.** ISBN 916. £2.95.

OLD MARGATE by **Michael David Mirams.** ISBN 908. £2.95.

OLD RAMSGATE by **Michael David Mirams.** ISBN 797. £2.95.

EXPLORING OLD ROCHESTER by **John Bryant.** A guide to buildings of historic interest. ISBN 827. £2.95.

THOMAS SIDNEY COOPER OF CANTERBURY by **Brian Stewart.** The life and work of Britain's best cattle painter, with 10 illustrations in colour. ISBN 762. £2.95.

A FIRST PICTUREBOOK OF OLD CHATHAM by **Philip MacDougall.** ISBN 754. £2.95.

A SECOND PICTUREBOOK OF OLD CHATHAM by **Philip MacDougall.** ISBN 924. £2.95.

CRANBROOK by **Jenni Rodger.** A pictorial history. ISBN 746. £2.95.

KENT TOWN CRAFTS by **Richard Filmer.** A pictorial record of sixteen different crafts. ISBN 584. £2.95.

KENTISH RURAL CRAFTS AND INDUSTRIES by **Richard Filmer.** A wide variety of rural crafts. ISBN 428. £2.50.

SMARDEN: A PICTORIAL HISTORY by **Jenni Rodger.** ISBN 592. £2.95.

A PICTUREBOOK OF OLD SHEPPEY by **Michael Thomas.** 130 Old photographs, mostly from glass negatives. ISBN 657. £2.95.

FIVE MEDWAY VILLAGES by **Wyn Bergess and Stephen Sage.** A pictorial history of Aylesford, Burham, Wouldham, Eccles and Borstal. ISBN 649. £2.95.

OLD SANDWICH by **Julian Arnold and Andrew Aubertin.** 146 old photographs. ISBN 673. £2.95.

AVIATION IN KENT by Robin Brooks. A pictorial history from 19th century ballooning to 1939. ISBN 681. £2.95.

A PICTURE BOOK OF OLD RAINHAM by Barbara Mackay Miller. ISBN 606. £2.95.

THE LIFE AND ART OF ONE MAN by Dudley Pout. A Kentish farmer's son who became successful as a commercial artist and as a children's illustrator. ISBN 525. £2.95.

OLD MAIDSTONE'S PUBLIC HOUSES by Irene Hales. 123 photographs. ISBN 533. £2.95.

OLD MAIDSTONE Vol. 1 by Irene Hales and Kay Baldock. ISBN 096. £2.50.

OLD MAIDSTONE Vol. 2 by Irene Hales. ISBN 38X. £2.50.

OLD ASHFORD by Richard Filmer. A photographic study of life in Ashford over 150 years. ISBN 72X. £2.95.

OLD TONBRIDGE by Don Skinner. ISBN 398. £2.50.

KENT TRANSPORT IN OLD POSTCARDS by Eric Baldock. 146 photographs. ISBN 320. £2.95.

GEORGE BARGEBRICK Esq. by Richard-Hugh Perks. The story of Smeed Dean Ltd in Sittingbourne. 80 illustrations. ISBN 479. £2.95.

STANDARD SIZE PAPERBACKS

EXPLORING KENT CHURCHES by John E. Vigar. What to look for when visiting a church. ISBN 3018. £3.95.

FLIGHT IN KENT. Another selection of articles by members of the Kent Aviation Historical Research Society. ISBN 3085. £1.95.

TALES OF VICTORIAN HEADCORN – see under hardbacks.

BIRDWATCHING IN KENT by Don Taylor. Details of when and where to watch for which birds, plus very readable accounts of personal experiences. ISBN 932. £4.50.

CRIME AND CRIMINALS IN VICTORIAN KENT by Adrian Gray. An insight into an intriguing if unsavoury side of Victorian life in Kent. ISBN 967. £3.95.

CHIDDINGSTONE – AN HISTORICAL EXPLORATION by Jill Newton. ISBN 940. £1.95.

STOUR VALLEY WALKS from Canterbury to Sandwich by Christopher Donaldson. Enjoy six days walking along the route taken by Caesar, Hengist & Horsa, St Augustine and many others. ISBN 991. £1.95.

THE GHOSTS OF KENT by Peter Underwood, President of the Ghost Club. ISBN 86X. £3.95.

CURIOUS KENT by John Vigar. A selection of the more unusual aspects of Kent history. ISBN 878. £1.95.

REAL ALE PUBS IN KENT by CAMRA in Kent. ISBN 894. £1.50.

A CHRONOLOGY OF ROCHESTER by Brenda Purle. ISBN 851. £1.50.

SITTINGBOURNE & KEMSLEY LIGHT RAILWAY STOCKBOOK AND GUIDE. ISBN 843. 95p.

DOVER REMEMBERED by Jessie Elizabeth Vine. Personal memories from the early years of this century. ISBN 819. £3.95.

THE PLACE NAMES OF KENT – see under hardbacks.

PENINSULA ROUND (The Hoo Peninsula) by Des Worsdale. ISBN 568. £1.50.

A HISTORY OF CHATHAM GRAMMAR SCHOOL FOR GIRLS, 1907-1982 by Audrey Perkyns. ISBN 576. £1.95.

CYCLE TOURS OF KENT by John Guy. No. 1: Medway, Gravesend, Sittingbourne and Sheppey. ISBN 517. £1.50.

THE CANTERBURY AND WHITSTABLE RAILWAY 1830-1980: A PICTORIAL SURVEY. ISBN 118. 75p.

ROCHESTER'S HERITAGE TRAIL. (Published for The City of Rochester Society.) A useful guide for the visitor to most places of interest in Rochester. ISBN 169. £1.25.

WINGS OVER KENT. A selection of articles by members of the Kent Aviation Historical Research Society. ISBN 69X. £1.95.

LULLINGSTONE PARK: THE EVOLUTION OF A MEDIAEVAL DEER PARK by Susan Pittman. ISBN 703. £3.95.

LET'S EXPLORE THE RIVER DARENT by Frederick Wood. Walking from Westerham to Dartford. ISBN 770. £1.95.

SAINT ANDREW'S CHURCH, DEAL by Gregory Holyoake. ISBN 835. 95p.

BIRDS OF KENT: A Review of their Status and Distribution. A reprint, with addendum, of the 448 page study by the Kent Ornithological Society. ISBN 800. £6.95.

Further titles are in preparation. Details will be announced in 'Bygone Kent'.